The Story of a Polish Exile

The Story of a Polish Exile

Witold Kasicki

ATHENA PRESS
LONDON

ISBN 10-digit 1 84401 836 9

ISBN 13-digit 978 1 84401 836 9

First Published 2007 by
ATHENA PRESS
Queen's House, 2 Holly Road
Twickenham TW1 4EG
United Kingdom

All names quoted are real and their stories could be substantiated
by collected documentation including letters, tapes and copies of
actual documents.

Printed for Athena Press

To my beloved wife, Maxine, my warrior princess. It was through your deep love, your steadfastness and your understanding of my so complex mind, and through the hours of talk and discussions, that the spoken word became the written one. Thank you Maxine for all your help and support. Our eyes say it all, but when written down that 'all' will become, for everyone to see, the proof of what we are.

Wituska

The author, just one year old – already with problems!

Introduction

I would like to dedicate this story to my beloved wife, Maxine. She certainly deserves this, as she has, for more than twenty years, been my love and my companion. We face the future knowing that whatever life brings we will manage it well together.

The trouble is that I do not know what that future is going to be. All I know for certain is that it will contain lots of potholes and setbacks but, at the same time, moments of happiness.

I always believed that I am not necessarily right, but that my aims are correct. If I had to make my *rachunek sumiena* (confession), I could say, with a very clear conscience, that the balance would be in my favour. I have never tried to make other people feel small because they were wrong, or at least not directly. However, I have always had a niggling feeling that such people must be told of their misbehaviour. Most of the time I succeeded – but alas, not always.

That is why I say this to Maxine, my dear wife: many times I have been difficult, awkward and impossible to understand, but I have always been loving, devoted and fully appreciative of what I have been given by you. I know that when I die, you will find some consolation that the years with me were not wasted. I hope you will be always happy.

In Poland before 1939

As my life nears slowly to the end, I have decided that the story of my past may be of some interest to many. Certainly for my mother it will fill gaps of those episodes that even she did not fully know. Also, I think my children and their families would be interested to learn who their father or grandfather is or was. There were many friends who were always close to me, who will be able to understand more what influenced my life and what actually made me into the person I am today.

I am dedicating this story to my present wife, Maxine, who has helped me so much. I can only say that she has already shown great interest, and I am sure that the reasons for my actions and reactions are now much clearer to her.

In writing my story, I have tried to be very honest – I have not concealed any facts that were not in my favour. I am, however, certain that there are many incidents that I have missed, which have become blurred in my mind. If the reader should find any inaccuracies or mistakes, I apologise in advance. After all, I am only human.

I have had many discussions with my parents, and lately with my mother, on the beginning of my life, and on the background of both my mother's and father's families. Except for my father's mother, whom I remember well, the rest of my grandparents died before I was one year old. My paternal grandmother lived in Warsaw, where she had a fashion salon. She was very good at this and her business thrived.

I don't know the occupation of my other grandparents, and I prefer not to speculate. All I do know is that my mother's father travelled twice to the USA, before the First World War, for a considerable time on each occasion, always returning with lots of presents for everyone. My father had one sister, and both he and she are now dead. My mother on the other hand was one of ten brothers and sisters. She was the youngest, with twenty years' difference between her and her oldest brother. So much so, that she was almost brought up by her older brothers. All of her nine siblings were well educated and have occupied very important positions, such as university professor, doctors, accountants, lawyers and teachers. I will be referring to them later in my story.

My father, who finished architectural college in Warsaw in 1916, was designated almost immediately after the end of the First World War to the rebuilding of Polish villages and stately homes destroyed and dilapidated through one hundred years of occupation and the war action before my country gained independence. He was sent to the middle part of Poland and there he eventually settled. How he and my mother found each other and fell in love, I do not know. However, my mother told me that she came to the same area after finishing teacher training college. She got her first job, as a teacher in the 'primary' school attached to a convent near Kielce. I have put primary in inverted commas as her pupils ranged between seven and well over twenty years of age. The reason for that was the fact that a lot of young people had missed their basic education either during the occupation or because they had been in the army during the First World War. For a young girl like my mother it was an extremely difficult job, especially as she was so isolated from the rest of her family and friends.

How she eventually met my father, as I said earlier, I don't know, but they must have been very happy in those early years, especially when they both settled in Jedrzejow.

At first they lived in a small flat near the station, and it was there I was born. I understand that the first years were very difficult, as my father had to travel a lot between different villages.

Eventually they moved to a bigger, semi-detached house in the town, which had a large garden and very nice neighbours, who became our friends for many years. They were Mr and Mrs Piekos. That friendship was very important in my upbringing as Mrs Piekos, or Pela, as I used to address her, was also a teacher and she actually taught me the basic principles of writing and counting. They did not have any children and I used to spend many afternoons at their house.

I always remember, when I rushed to my mother saying, 'Mum, I can already write my own name.' I developed very quickly into a fine young boy.

As my father's job was picking up very well indeed, we travelled a lot in the countryside, in a large landau with a pair of horses and a driver. This went with my father's job; the distances covered by his frequent visits from village to village, and some stately homes, would run into many miles.

The middle part of Poland retained its social structure and was least affected by the occupation forces, whether Russian, German, Austrian or Hungarian. The result was that the peasantry were still run by the remaining Polish magnates. Those magnates were always in contact with the West, from where the greatest influence of culture affected our lives. That part of Poland greatly favoured contact with the western world.

To what extent my life has been affected by the social life of my country, by my education, the literature, the religion and its very turbulent history, I will try to describe later in my story. This, however, will only be based on the facts as I have seen and experienced then. As this is my story, I feel, it is right to give it my interpretation even if some people might not agree with me.

As I said earlier, my parents started at the bottom of their respective professional ladders, and through hard work they established themselves quite well and relatively quickly.

We managed to travel a lot as a family. When I was three, we went to the Baltic Sea, visited ports and went to an open-air opera at the very famous amphitheatre in Wejherowo, near Gdansk. I don't remember much about it, but from various tales I know that this opera finished as a great fiasco, because of heavy rain and a storm that damaged everything, although this might have been rather appropriate as the performance was Wagner's *Die Walküre*!

When I was five, we visited my grandmother's house in Warsaw. I was taken to the Grand Opera House to the famous Polish ballet, *Pan Twardowski*. This I remember quite well to this day. I also remember going with my grandmother to the big market, where she wanted to buy me a large football; but I refused saying that my father would buy me a proper one later.

We also travelled many times to visit my mother's brothers and sisters, but as they were much better off, I felt that we were treated as 'poor relations' and I was dismayed at such an attitude. I was never good company on such occasions, with one exception – when I was visiting Aunt Hela in Cracow. I stayed with my Aunt Hela in Cracow for the first three years whilst studying on an engineering course at college. This I will describe later.

In principle, I was a very good child, but there were moments when the 'other' side of me prevailed. When I was about two or three years old, I used to play with the other children in sandpits, collecting all sorts of things, including large toads, and bringing them to my mother. Her fright at the sight of the spitting toads is still very much in my mind.

When I was slightly older, my friend and I played with toys like bows and arrows. There would normally be a duel, until on one occasion my arrow almost removed the eye of my opponent. However, he had his revenge on me, when we played hide-and-seek one time. I was hidden in the empty rainwater barrel, not answering to his calls, and he eventually threw a brick with rather poor results for my head!

We used to have two dogs around that time; one for hunting, and the other was my pet fox terrier, who was called *Iskra* (Sparkle in English). The hunting dog was always lazy, basking in the sun, but Sparkle was always active. I remember how many times she escaped the dog catcher. As she was a very clever dog she would organise on every Sunday a procession of other dogs from the neighbourhood, to escort the dog catcher and his family to the church. She was certainly not his favourite dog.

Once one of us brought a pregnant hedgehog home. There was no chance for anyone to send it away. Every night we were woken up by the tip-tap of her feet, hedgehogs being nocturnal creatures. Unfortunately, when about twelve pinkish hedgehogs were born, they were all killed by Sparkle. A very sad story!

I should say that the first years were extremely happy for us.

I have been told that when I was one year old and on a picnic with my parents, I was left in the clearing of a wood in the care of my beloved fox terrier, who incidentally was the same age as myself. My parents were picking berries and mushrooms in the forest, when the growling of my dog made them run to rescue me, but upon seeing a large deer standing over me, my father stopped and stood very still until the deer moved away, being frightened that I might be trodden on.

When I was perhaps between two and three years old, I was very ill with diphtheria. In those days you could not be inoculated against this dreadful illness. I remember when the curtains were half-drawn and our friend Dr Przybkowski arrived. My tummy was exposed and a great syringe appeared, filled with serum, which was injected directly into my stomach.

I do not remember whether I cried or not, but due to high temperature or possibly my already very imaginative mind, for a few days I saw various scenes of animals, people or creatures, all horrible. This I remember vividly.

Dr Przybkowski used to come to us very often. He had three hobbies; radios, clocks and astronomy. The first one, radios, were in a very early stage of development in the world, straight from the crystal set that I was given probably when I was five or six years old. But I was already fascinated with the doctor's radios, which were enormous, with about ten to twelve valves, all very large, in a box, which would be clad internally with mirrors, so that he could see every joint. I did not, I must confess, remember ever hearing it playing even once, but it was just his hobby.

As mentioned, clocks were another very serious hobby for him. I remember begging my parents to go to see Dr Przybkowski at noon. There were practically all sorts of chiming clocks. It was his ambition that all would chime simultaneously. You can imagine the effect on a small boy. I had already a great musical ear, so I was told. I was in a paradise there. Grandfather clocks, grandmother clocks, the very old ones with one hand only and no casing; some had beautiful faces inlaid with mother-of-pearl, and some were very mysterious in shape. I would have spent hours there, if only I was allowed.

Since then, because of my great interest in clocks, I have seen many of them in different houses and museums, and I even used to make some. This means I used to buy old French type movements and design the casing for them, usually in beautiful wood. We still have one left in our house, and one in my son's house. Dr Przybkowski's son donated his father's collection of clocks to Cracow Museum, where they are admired even today by millions of visitors. Cracow was hardly damaged during the Second World War.

The third hobby of Dr Przybkowski, and that I know mostly from my parents' and friends' stories much later, was his astronomical observatory, which was installed in the specially constructed turret on the roof of his house in Jedrzejow. There he would study the stars, not unlike today's radio and television personality Patrick Moore. However, the story goes that every Sunday he would lower his telescope and direct it to the nearby woodland.

I was told later that with the cooperation of his wife, not unlike residents of our village of Ixworth, he would inform the rest of our small town of the latest news! But enough of that.

I do not know when he had time to practice his medicine, but he saved not only my life, but the likes of many others also, very efficiently. A great man.

Also, whilst I was living in Jedrzejow, when I was nearing six years old, my father woke me up around midnight. I was dressed and ushered to the marketplace, where by that time scores of people were gathering, almost filling the entire square. The reason for such attraction was a fire. My town, although not very large (say 10,000 to 12,000 souls), was quite industrial in its character. The building that was on fire was a four-storey, perhaps one hundred-foot frontage warehouse containing ironmongery, paper, paints and structural steel. Because the various kinds of paint were stored in the basement and, I was told, that was where the fire had started, by the time my father and I arrived, the whole building was fully engulfed in flames. The firemen could only protect the adjoining properties. The fire raged for two days and nights. Everything was completely burnt or melted, including the copper, brass and steel. There were numerous explosions, caused by big drums bursting with the heat. The paint, I was told, was the greatest enemy. But what I, a six-year-old child, would remember was the picture of the whole colourful scene. There was a complete rainbow of colours, which reflected in the windows on the other side of the square and in the faces of all the other people, and in the sky. This I will never forget. It was the picture I always wanted to paint but it has never materialised.

During this time, as I have already mentioned earlier, my father was a great hunter, fisherman and naturalist. I do not know how one links this desire to kill animals and at the same time to be their greatest lover. There was an incident when I was nearly drowned in a very large pond, covered with water lilies and reeds. There were millions of fish, and the whole area was surrounded by marshland. I was probably six or seven years old, and my father was hunting wild ducks. I was left with my fishing rod and a small bore rifle (you will discover from my later recollection, that on all Boy Scout camps, we were always armed for night watches with small bore rifles, fully loaded with live ammunition. We had our training on small ranges very early in life. We knew all the rules and I do not ever remember any accidents, neither do I remember if the rifle was ever used on our camps). But to return to my story, I was very happily fishing in the pond, where within a very few minutes I caught several large carp. I happily brought them to our quarters but when I described where I had had such luck, my father and his companion took the fish away from me, and delivered it back to the pond – apparently, the owner had been breeding carp in that pond. Fortunately the fish were still alive, but my father confiscated my fishing rod.

I was then left with the rifle, and was told to be very careful in the marshes. You had to jump from one tussock of grass to the next one, but I slipped and what saved my life was my rifle, which formed a bridge, allowing me to climb back very clumsily. That taught me a good lesson. Nevertheless, I proceeded to a spot where a few local boys were enjoying themselves in a very curious sport. There was a very deep area at the other pond, and the boys were diving at the edge and from time to time they would emerge with a fish – sturgeon. The fish would shelter, deep in the water, along the side of the bank. The skill of those boys was fantastic.

Then I swam in between the water lilies and reeds – it was lovely, the water and the sun were very hot. Unfortunately, my arm got entangled into the roots of the water lilies, but as I was already quite a good swimmer I managed to untangle my arms, turned on my back and screamed for help. Those same boys arrived and helped me out – this was my other lesson.

There was a third lesson in what was an otherwise a beautiful extended weekend. My father allowed me to borrow his shotgun for a while. Watching me all the time, he pointed to black crows in the sky. I was not yet very strong; therefore, he placed a kind of padding on my shoulder and asked me to lie down – face up, of course. He told me to point the gun at the birds and shoot, which I did, feeling rather a great pain in my shoulder (this did not matter to me). Something fell down – I had hit a bird. I ran as fast as I could, and found it was a small hawk – unfortunately, mortally wounded. However, it managed to embed all its talons in my hand. I screamed and my father ran to me and killed the hawk, but worse was to come. I was taken as quickly as possible to the local doctor, who, after giving me some injections, had to remove every single claw, one by one. That was rather an unfortunate finish to my short holiday, and it took me a whole week to recover.

I must add that my father shot on this occasion between ten and twenty wild ducks. On some other occasions when I was not present he would bring home ten or more hares, ducks, foxes, and even wild boar.

There were several very amusing incidents with my dog Sparkle. As I said earlier, she was given to my father as a present by the breeder of fox hunting dogs (fox terriers). She was born on the same day as I.

Sparkle was mated once on the same breeding farm that she had come from, and she gave birth to three puppies. One was given to my Aunt Marysia, who trained this dog to be like a circus dog (my aunt did not have any children). I don't remember the dog's name, but if you would say 'Judy', or whatever her name was, 'you have a headache', she would walk on her hind legs, keeping her front legs on her head, several times round the table. Her sense of smell was phenomenal – you could hide anything after offering her the item to sniff, and it would take only seconds for her to find where it was hidden. She knew dozens of tricks – though I don't necessarily approve of that!

Coming back to Sparkle, she adored me and this was reciprocated. She was a rather naughty little dog. We had a young boy delivering papers every morning, which she hated, and one morning she tore his trousers. Sparkle was reported and the case was brought before the magistrate. This was a small town and everyone knew each other. At this time we still had Sparkle's daughter, who was almost identical. My father knew the defending lawyer and they decided on a kind of trick.

The defence brought Sparkle to the court and asked the boy whether this was the dog that had attacked him. 'Yes, Your Honour,' he replied. Then they withdrew Sparkle, and her daughter was brought in. 'Is this the dog which attacked you – are you sure?'

'Yes, Your Honour,' the youth again replied. After that he was confronted with both dogs, which of course, he could not distinguish. The case was dismissed, but I have been told that my father sent the boy a new pair of trousers anyway.

When we moved to Kielce after some years – I think in 1936, when she would have been sixteen years old – she was run over by a lorry. It was a sad goodbye to a great friend.

Another family incident happened when we were still in Jedrzejow. There was a huge mulberry tree near one corner of our house. During April, which is the cats' month for mating, there was, right after midnight, a colossal commotion with meowing in the mulberry tree. My father was so annoyed at the noise that he took his shotgun and fired it at the tree. He missed, of course, but you could imagine the upheaval in Lysakowska Street. Everybody was talking about it for days afterwards.

My father and Mr Piekos used to meet very often. There would be endless discussions on political and social matters, and many times only a good drink of vodka could solve the arguments. But it was a very happy relationship. I remember well Pela, his wife – she was a very good lady.

Besides playing with my dog, going hunting with my father and having dangerous games, I also enjoyed other activities, which for years gave me a lot of pleasure and satisfaction. From my youngest days, my father, seeing that I was quite a naturalist (and he himself was very good at that, he could imitate almost all birds and wild animals), he made two things for me. The first was a net for catching butterflies or beetles, or even the large horned beetle. Secondly I was given a bottle like a jam jar, in which there was cotton wool at the bottom saturated with ether, and a bottle of ether. I don't suppose you could get that in a chemist's shop today. Also at home there was, again made by my father, a small frame for shaping the collection of caught insects, before being mounted in a glass case. He, of course, told me how to do it, from start to finish.

I was told that catching insects was not so difficult, but to collect them without damaging them was another matter. But with the ether rapidly evaporating, any moth or butterfly put into the jar would die instantly. Then, as soon as possible, the insect should be very carefully spread on the prepared frame. Afterwards the insects were sorted out and placed in a flat display case, with names, places and dates.

I also collected caterpillars of various moths and butterflies, and kept them in cardboard boxes with the sort of food they were used to. There would, of course, be an adequate number of holes for air. From time to time I would climb to the top of the wardrobe, where the boxes were kept, to check the supply of food and to see whether the change into the cocoon stage had occurred. One day some time later we would be woken up by the new butterfly or moth. What an excitement! My mother was not always excited, especially if she would be woken up in the middle of the night. 'Witold, take it away, take it away,' she would shout. My mother was always afraid of moths, spiders, mice and such like. Not me!

In my young days I learnt a lot from my parents. Perhaps more from my father because he was then more at home, as my mother was teaching (later she retired when she was sick, although she was still very young). She became ill with the beginnings of TB, and she would often have to be in the sanatorium. I would not see her very much.

Anyway, another thing that I learnt early in life, which was started by my father, was stamp collecting. It was, of course, done very properly. I had two albums, one totally devoted to Polish stamps, and the other to stamps from the rest of the world. Poland was probably influenced by Germany in that field of hobbies. Germany paid a vast proportion of their compensation for their action in the First World War in the form of stamp collections. The other aspect was that the Polish collection contained a very large number of stamps, from before, during and after that war – the reason being that Poland was under various occupations. Polish or occupying authorities were using our stamps and over-stamping them again with different denominations of money, like Deutschmarks or Pfennig, or roubles, or including signs of the country, like the two-headed black eagles for Germany. These over-stamped stamps were very valuable, particularly the ones with mistakes, like being upside-down or half way across the sheet of stamps. I would also collect envelopes giving the date – these were very valuable too. I had postal stamps that were over-stamped twice. The very curious ones were when just after the First World War, there was a colossal devaluation in Germany, and there were stamps again over-stamped with values of up to 5,000,000 marks.

Incidentally, my uncle in Cracow told me that at this time he had been collecting his salary in millions of marks – so much so that he would take an empty suitcase to collect his salary on the last day of the month! The money was completely worthless – in the end they used it for lighting open fires!

This was also a time when I read dozens of books, including biographical works and detective stories like those of Conan Doyle. I was not allowed to read late in bed, so I had my torchlight hidden under the eiderdown, and one night would be sufficient for one crime book. Probably, this is common today too.

As a postscript to the last stories, I know that my mother, before coming to England, sold my stamp collection, butterfly collection, cello, and many other items, as she was unable to take these things to England with her.

I will continue with my young days, as the scene I will describe has not to my knowledge been watched by a six-year-old.

Most people know all the wildfowl, like peacocks, black grouse (black cock), etc. But I wonder how many have been watching them when mating. This is the story that I had in mind when I described the phenomenon that my father would adore wild animals, birds and fish, yet would hunt them in the appropriate season. He, however, is not an exception; my son-in-law almost completely lost his hearing, in one ear, by shooting without earmuffs for such birds. This is a passion. Anyway, I was, at six years old, included in the party, early in the spring, to a selected hideout, from where one could watch the magnificent performances by males to woo their partners. The plumage was a beautiful display, and the courtship dance would last for hours. I was a very young boy, but I learnt a lot! There were all the different species in various hideouts, and these were in the grounds of the Radziwilow estate. I have been privileged to be invited to a luncheon party in their mansion, where the food was of the best quality and one would have to learn how to eat it (with the help of the waiters). I wonder whether Jackie Kennedy was there as a small girl?

I always liked nature and I always admired the natural

selection of the species, of which I learnt later during my education.

I was bewildered when travelling with my father in the landau on the occasion of Good Friday, when we would stop on the way at a vicarage known to my father. The village vicar would come out with greetings. We would be ushered into his study; his words as I well remember were, 'Now you are travelling, therefore, you are excused from fasting, and I certainly would not have my guest dining without company. Which turkey should we have for lunch?'

He would promptly take his shotgun, open the window looking on to the yard, select the bird, and with a bang, our meal would be ready in a few hours! The housekeeper would see to that. Then his huge cupboard would be opened; it would be full of drinks, sausages, hams, etc., and elevenses would be served. I was excused from drinking (which I first started when I was twenty-two years old), but other goodies were fine for me! The day ended happily, and next morning we departed for our destination. What an ironical life when even after one hundred years of the occupation of Poland people have not improved their bad habits.

I could still tell stories connected with the first decade of my life – but before we leave Jedrzejow, I must recall one day when we were returning home from a day's hunting. My father was telling me a story about the huge carts that carried hay or corn, which returned home after dusk. Usually at this time the drivers were very tired, and the horses pulling the carts would normally find their own way home. Therefore, the drivers would fall asleep. Often the scythe would be pushed into the hay at the side of the cart. Once, however, a motorbike driver, unaware, overtook such a cart and lost his head in the process – what a thought!

When I was seven years old, we moved to Kielce, where my father started his own practice as architect/engineer. He was responsible for many projects, so much so, that some streets in Kielce were almost entirely designed by him. People would call them Kasicki Streets, tongue-in-cheek.

Also, at this time, by law I had to attend primary school. It was unfortunate the school chosen by my mother was a girls' school. I escaped home after the first hour of being introduced to this school. My mother, of course, brought me back, with me crying. I managed to stay in this school for one year, achieving the best possible certificate, at the end of the year.

The next school I considered better, as it was at least a boys' school, with a high standard of education.

Kielce was a district town, with a population of 130,000 people and a long history, as it had been a bishop's town for generations. It had a great palace, cathedral, monastery and a huge marketplace to where the peasant women would twice a week walk for miles to bring their 'goodies' – home-made cheese, birds (dead or alive), even calves, and all kinds of vegetables. As the women wanted to look their best, they would wear the traditional costumes, but to save on shoes they would walk barefoot, wash their feet in the last stream, and then put their shoes back on, ready for their entry to the town.

At the market there would be much bargaining. This would include checking the age of the hen or fowl by the colour of its feet, etc. Once my father's mother took me to the market, together with a sack, without explaining the reason.

Shortly, I realised that she intended to bargain for a live piglet. The bargain was struck, and I, with the live piglet wriggling frantically in the sack, was walking on the road furthest from the town, so that I would not be spotted by any of my friends. This road led over a very narrow road bridge, very high above the river. I arrived home and that was the end of my contribution.

Once, however, I was asked to kill a chicken. My mother said, 'Just go to the basement and cut off its head.' What I was not told was that by cutting the head off the hen, you do not kill the bird. After I cut the head off, the rest of the body was dancing round the cellar – I was covered in blood and ran out. I have never killed anything or anybody since that time, even during my time in the concentration camp or during war. I still have now some inborn idiosyncrasy that I even hesitate to kill a spider. You may think I am a pacifist – no. I only experienced something in my early life, which left its mark on me to this day.

But coming back to special events – fire again. I was probably eight years old, when I was again woken up at three or four in the morning, told to get dressed quickly, and we went across Kielce. It was winter, with a temperature of -33 °C. There must have been rain the day before, because the roads and pavements were like a skating rink. We could hardly climb to the top of the road, where the cathedral was. I fell several times, but eventually by reaching the top we could see in the distance an enormous fire. It was from one of the largest timber yards, which was fully ablaze. The whole horizon was filled with the fire and smoke. We walked some distance to that area, which fortunately was separated from the rest of the town by the river; but as far as I remember it, it lasted for days – no one could save anything from the fire. It was strangely contradictory, as when coming nearer to the timber yard, the heat was terrific, yet the scarf wrapped round my face and ears had to stay on because, as I said earlier the frost was below -33 °C, and I could easily have lost an ear or a nose. I have seen many such tragedies much later on when the German soldiers were returning from Stalingrad.

Nevertheless, such a fire – even if I have seen worse later on, was imprinted in my memory for many years to come. I remember how my mother had opposed my going to see the fire, but I was thankful to my father for taking me.

In the early years in Kielce, I was assessed as a tuberculosis case. I remember the doctor looking at my eyes, saying, 'These eyelashes are the true indication of my theory.' I was sent to a sanatorium in the Polish Tatra Mountains for one month, and I spent another month with my mother in nearby Rabka. It was lovely to fish for salmon, by using a handkerchief knotted at each corner as an inverted parachute. I used to catch many small salmon, until I was found out. In the sanatorium, life was quite nice, but very strict. I have a photograph of us sitting around the fire outside and having some kind of barbecue.

This was the place where I entered into a kind of competition – who could eat the most buns for breakfast. I lost, but only because there were not any more buns left. The place was very well organised, but I always had the suspicion that the 'ladies' were spying on us, and it was, I am sure, to creep and uncover our lower parts, checking our activities with our 'private quarters' – the big smack they administered on our bottoms must have given them much pleasure.

On coming back to Kielce I found that my mother was suffering from a kind of tuberculosis, and she was sent to a sanatorium in the Tatra Mountains too. I was left with my father, who was certainly no cook, therefore he arranged with a local restaurant that I could come in and order lunch to my liking. That was great! I would order soup, tripe with pulpit and some dessert. I felt very independent. I didn't know what my father spent his time doing, but I wasn't interested in any case.

Probably much too early and without experience, I innocently got involved in a game with sexual connotations. We always had a maid at home, and she had a little room next to the bathroom and kitchen. That was disastrous, as she could watch me through a high-level window between her room and the bathroom. She lured me to climb to her room for a game. She was probably ten years older than I. It was a game, but being very young, it left me thinking about it for a long time. Those peasant girls were very innocent, but very sensual. She taught me a lot, but fortunately no one discovered anything.

You have already read about my experiences during my first year of primary school, which was for girls, from which I ran away, just to be brought back. As you know, after one year I had top colours and I was the top boy (there was no top girl).

It was a relief in the second year when I joined a proper boys' school. I was not at the top at the end of my time there, but I had many experiences there. Nothing was extraordinary and nothing really got imprinted on my memory.

Eleven-plus, and I was admitted to the Grammar School of Brothers Sniadecki. The school is still there, and so I have to be very careful to describe some extraordinary scenes during my eight years there. One thing I can say that these were the most successful years in my whole life.

I remember it was the first day after the entrance examination, when we all looked at the board to see whether our names were there – and whether we knew our companions. I passed, but I hardly knew anyone from my form. Later, I found that there were sons of two doctors, one professor of a local college and one judge, whose son was born in Tibet. There were two boys from Swietokrzyskie-gory, sons of very radical politicians. There was a film addict, and there was one boy who could perform tap-dancing like the best of the Hollywood stars. Twenty-nine or thirty boys from all walks of life, and yet as my mind wanders back over those eight years we have grown into a very diverse but otherwise unique group, who would do anything under the motto of the three musketeers, 'one for all and all for one'. The life in the grammar school definitely shaped our characters and gave us the ability to use our talents to the full.

I would not say that all of us could cope with both the study and the social life. There were those whose background was seriously radical.

I was always a strong and healthy boy. From the first year of grammar school I joined the scouts. Year after year I would be active in this movement. I had nearly eighty badges and nearly all grades in the scouting movement. Twice a year we would go camping, as I have already said, in the lowlands and lakes, in the two months of the summer vacations, and in the Polish Tatra Mountains for one or two weeks in the winter.

When I later became Commissioner, I was given a

very smart uniform by my parents. I was very proud of it, and I would wear it whenever possible. To be given the right to wear this uniform was almost the greatest distinction there was in the scouting movement.

I do not think there was any sport I did not enjoy. Trekking, swimming, skating, skiing, volleyball, basketball nearly every day, but the most enjoyable was cycling. I got my first and last bicycle when I went to grammar school. This bicycle lasted me seven years; it was a semi-racer with three gears. Every day I would cycle to school, and it was two miles. I knew this cycle in every part. Once, I even raced with the 'puffy-train', and won. The road ran parallel with the train track, and the train driver congratulated me, as it was a distance of ten miles.

At school, physics, chemistry and handiwork were my best subjects. I used to prepare all the experiments the day before, for the whole form; in fact, my best friend Mietek and I got the keys to the school and all laboratories. We stayed several times up to 10 p.m., but the caretaker would send us home. As there were no hooligans then, my parents did not worry about me coming home late.

Once, I remember, when I was fourteen or fifteen years old, Mietek and I tried to repair a burnt-out dynamo, which was a large school machine, used for many experiments. It was a big job! The school provided us with extra-insulated wire and evening after evening we designed how to wind the rotor of the motor, and how to solder the connections to the collector. We succeeded – hurrah – but only in securing the coils in their grooves.

Professor Michniak was a good man, he was so excited he could not wait for the safety slips to be put in. 'Try switching it on,' he said. Sadly all the wires, which had been so carefully wound up, flew away. But believe it or not, we did the whole job again, and this time, to our great satisfaction it worked.

Professor Michniak was not only a good teacher; he was also a scientist. Both Mietek and I used to go to him and talk about chemistry, about the new discoveries like Rentgen, Rad and Polon. We talked about Maria Sklodowska (Marie Curie), about her work on radium. Our professor was the first person to tell us how she had given to her country, Poland, twelve grams of radium (which is still in use, at the Polish Institute, named after her). He also told us of his great interest in the quantum theory. It was fascinating to talk to the old man.

When we learnt electronics, we saw the cinema film, *Bride of Frankenstein*, and we decided, Mietek and I, to try and catch thunder and lightning. Mietek lived not more than 200 yards from me, and there were fields and a river not far away. Therefore, we built a huge kite out of tinfoil, fixed one large earthing point into the ground, with a ten-millimetre ball at the top, and above it, well constructed, another ball with a ten-centimetre gap between them. To the top ball we connected thin, insulated wire and put the kite to work, not forgetting to ensure that a storm was coming. Certainly, the storm came, and I do not think I have ever seen such lightning before. Of course, the kite and all the wires completely disappeared. How we survived, I do not know.

We liked the experiments in the physics and chemistry laboratories. When the enormous electrostatic machine, (some one and a half metres in diameter) was put in rotation, then the whole form would join hands and the last ones would touch the polar ends of the machine. The effect was fantastic; we felt the sparkles coming between our fingers, shaking badly. It was a lovely experience!

Our pack of thirty was formed, as I said earlier, from completely different backgrounds, some very colourful and original, whose parents made money either by inheritance, or by being good businessmen. The result of this expressed itself in very heated debates, but always orderly, whether chaired by the form top boy or by the form master.

This brings me to the way the school was run. It was a rather old building, which had formerly housed a commercial school. We always preferred to forget that fact. There were two other grammar schools in Kielce, similar to ours. However, there was a difference, both in teaching methods and their social structure. The school outside the town was Roman Catholic and run by Jesuits. It was most popular with the majority of people in town. It was called 'Bishop's School', and this did not help. The other school was very good – the famous Polish writer Zeromski was a pupil – and was favoured by upper classes, the so-called intelligentsia. Then there was our school, which was of course the best. It catered for all social groups, was well organised both by the staff and by the self-governing council of boys at all levels.

I always regret that Ingrid, my daughter, went to St Ursula's Convent School. We had been misinformed, as there were two such schools in London. The other one in west London, we discovered later, had had a much better reputation – I have, perhaps, now even more imprinted in me that the schools cannot and should not be run by monks or nuns.

One remembers the history of the inquisition, and the absurd obsession to place religion, by force if necessary, as the basis of our education. Religion, which is to be based on belief, usually comes later in life, and then it is very much more firmly embedded in us. We could fight to defend our beliefs, but we turn away from something which is also called 'belief', but it is gradually implanted almost by force, or by threats. One must not generalise such statements, but one must be aware of their existence.

Let's return to the organisation of our school. It was like all grammar schools in Poland, being paid for by the parents, but it was not a proper fee-paying school. The amount of money was very nominal. One must remember that our country was just beginning to stand firmly on its own two feet again. However, there existed hardships and many boys would be allowed to study free, and go on holiday free too.

The qualification for free study – or study at a reduced fee – was discussed at all levels of the school hierarchy. Parents would apply to the director and he would have discretional powers to grant such free education. Even the form master, with the cooperation of the governing body of each form, could apply his power to persuade the director to grant a reduction in fees for one or two boys. I knew of cases where the boys concerned or their parents would not even know about it.

Our director, or headmaster, came from the upper middle class. He was always correctly dressed and knew almost all the boys by their surnames or first names. He was extremely respected by everybody in the school. He was not very old, but his first wife died and he married a lady much younger than himself. She too was highly respected – perhaps because of her age, she felt nearer to us. She often helped to organise different events.

The staff were varied. There were a number of old

teachers, with high qualifications. There were also many younger ones who went through the First World War, who were bursting with patriotic feelings, which were felt by all of us. However, the patriotic feelings differed, sometimes very much, having the same aims but springing from both socialistic/radical ideas and very conservative ones. One has to remember that Poland was occupied for one hundred years by three powers: Russia, the Austro-Hungarian Empire and Germany. Russia became communist, and the new ideology influenced many Poles. It was actually touch-and-go as to who would be first at the helm of the new Poland. Legiony (the new army formed by General Pilsudski, who was for years imprisoned in the Warsaw Citadel and in Elba) was freed just in time to produce his 'miracle', and he became leader of this country of some 36 million people. The treaty of Versailles will be long remembered in Poland.

Therefore, those who followed Pilsudski spread their influence in all walks of Polish life. So it happened that we had many such teachers – some with a good education, some with a less good one. However, all were pounding into us the idea of rebuilding our ruined country. Although many of them would have been educated in Austria, Russia or Germany, the idea of rebuilding Poland was always on their lips.

Our school catered for everybody in accordance with their ability. Only the final matriculation exams were set out by the team of professors at the Ministry of Education. (Actually my mother's second oldest brother was one of such men.) They would also travel throughout the country, bringing the examination papers in sealed envelopes, and they would supervise the examination procedure.

Let me now describe the organisation of our school, which was not dissimilar in other schools.

There were usually three to four first-form classes, gradually reducing to one form at the eighth level, which in later years became two-year lyceum. The school was governed by the director with a team of teachers.

Every form, from day one, would organise a self-determining body, who would choose their leader (the head boy of the form). We would have one hour per week, when no one from the staff would be present, and we ourselves, under the leadership of our head boy, could choose the subjects for discussion. They would all be noted by the head boy, who would pass the resolution to the form master, and to the head boy of the school. There would be an additional hour when the form master would be in the chair. Obviously, in the first three to four years it was not too serious. After all, we started at the age of eleven. However, with the careful guidance of the form master, our experience in this self-governing body would grow, and at a later stage we would have a greater say in not only the running of our social life, but also in our education. One could write books on this subject, especially for a country like Britain, where only some who benefit from secondary education reach high positions in governing the country, and only a small proportion of them, mainly unionists, could beat the others punch for punch in expressing their opinions. Unfortunately, this became a political issue, where those who 'have' are on one side of the House of Commons and those who 'have not' are on the other side. Perhaps even in this country, gradually, as we are already observing, that anomaly will disappear for everyone's benefit.

As far as learning was concerned, there were syllabi, as there are in every school, but perhaps we had greater influence on stressing the importance of this or that subject. We learnt literature, geography, history, biology, etc., by considering every problem, through the ages, of countries and cultures. And here I come to the subject with which I began to talk about education – the influence of religion. Poland is almost totally a Roman Catholic country. Even in the present situation where the Soviets have banned religion being taught in the schools, many party members are sending their children to Sunday schools, to churches to be baptised and confirmed. However, this may be rather a controversial issue. Catholicism in Poland is taken for granted.

I'll give an example: in our school for the first two years we had as our religion teacher a local vicar – rather overweight, but a very nice man otherwise. All he taught us were psalms, and some parables from the New Testament. We knew in advance which psalms would be for the following week – therefore, we elected one boy to write all the words on a sheet and we would pin it to the side of the 'cathedra seat', as we used to call the boxed platform where the teacher would sit.

The results, of course, were beyond belief – everyone got five (we have four grades, five being top, four, three, two, and one being a failure) To me it was unbelievable that this was never discovered.

Unfortunately, he retired, and we then got a new young priest – Dr Lapot, a very learned clergyman.

Dr Lapot was simply appalled by what we had been doing as religious education. We had to do three years' study in one year. And here I must stress that in Poland, unlike Britain, you would not be allowed to the next form if one of your subjects was a failure, whether it was religion or handiwork. At first we hated that man, but he was so intelligent that by matriculation level we were experts not only in Roman Catholic teaching but in all comparative religions. I did not mean that we finished fully conversant in Roman Catholic beliefs, but we could enter in any discussion on that subject. I was basically a good Roman Catholic, but we have had numerous discussions on religion, which as everyone knows is a very difficult subject. Fortunately, for the last five years of the grammar school, our comparative religion was extremely good and helped us to form our opinion that everybody has a right to belong to his or her own religion. We had Jews and Russian Orthodox, who would be released from attending our Roman Catholic lessons, but who would have to produce at the end of the term the certificate signed by their respective teachers of religion, proving that they had reached the required standard.

Most of us were practising – that was not compulsory – except for Sunday Mass, at 10 a.m. in our cathedral. We marched together through the town after the list was read and checked. We treated it as a duty. This helped us in crystallising our characters. When in the upper forms, it usually ended with asking your girlfriend for a friendly walk in the park. That was allowed! But everyone, boys and girls, always wore school uniform, and if a report reached the director of any misbehaviour it could mean expulsion – and the so-called 'Woolf's letter' – so that no other school would dare accept you.

'Woolf's letter' was a great incentive to our self-governing body to take care of the unruly characters, especially when in the last school years their political activities were outside the control of the self-governing body of students or teachers. In this case I refer to the growing anti-Semitism, as an example of this. Don't forget that out of 36 million people living in Poland, there were 4.5 million Jews, nearly 3 million Ukrainians (they were mostly on the South Russian border) and 2 million Germans (they were left behind after the First World War, near the eastern border). There were a few million Belorussleaya people, (white Russians, but not to be confused with the white Russians who were anti-communist). There were Czechs, Lithuanians, Latvians, etc. I think there were some 40 per cent of minorities, and it was very difficult to control such a conglomeration of peoples. In our school we had discussions and many times some pressure would have to be exerted to keep such characters at bay. When one thinks that all but three students arrived at matriculation level in our group, this must be considered a good achievement by any standard.

As I was saying earlier, I was one of the first to organise the scouting movement at our school, with the help of the school authorities, and some other enterprises (we never held jumble sales or any sponsored events). We were able to purchase complete camping equipment for about ninety boys. I don't remember how many patrols we had, but I was in the fourth form when I was captain of some 120 Boy Scouts. The school offered us a large room for our headquarters, with cupboards and tables. Glass cupboards were very important, to store our trophies. There was one small problem with this room – it was adjoining the main conference room, where the individual students and their future would be discussed by the teaching body; the final decision on marking and opinions would be given by the teachers. There was a door, which was fully padded, providing protection against unlawful listening in advance of any such information. I cannot tell you how often I was approached, and with how many ideas, about breaking that rule. It never succeeded and that was one of my great prides. You must remember that in the late twenties or even the early thirties, there were no minute microphones and I was actually the most knowledgeable person in electronics. As I explained earlier, my best subjects were physics, chemistry, art and workshop work. Therefore, I was subject to various temptations to break that rule, but 'No' was always my answer. 'I was given that room for my scouts on trust, and I will never break it.'

When I was talking of our training in the workshops, this incorporated all 'trades'. We were very lucky to have such a well-equipped section that could prepare us for all sorts of jobs – from simple factory worker to great scientist. It was probably thanks to the quality of our teachers that we were inspired to such abilities, to fulfil ourselves to the utmost. It was also the fact that, with much more primitiveness in the twenties and thirties, everything was done to utilise all available equipment to the maximum, with the students' help of course, so that all the techniques known could be conveyed to the students. Who would nowadays think that a student like me at the age of fourteen or fifteen years, would be given the task of building a twenty-four-volt generator completely from scratch? Firstly designing the machine, then building it step by step, constructing big electromagnets like a big horseshoe (measuring twelve inches square), making bobbins and winding the insulated copper wire, making a rotor from thin sheets of steel and again winding the wires and soldering them to the earlier constructed collector.

Then to make life a little more difficult, threading the axle and making ball bearings, with the exception of the steel balls. Eventually, I mounted the whole thing on a heavy, hardwood base. If I would tell you that I have seen my dynamo working on a visit to Poland, while revisiting my school, in 1976 (that is, forty years after making it), you could understand how proud I was! This, of course, was one of many projects, which I constructed during my eight years of grammar school. Some were in wood, some glass, some electronics. As a postscript, I could add that thanks to our treadle-lathe I could help myself in the concentration camp, volunteering to work an electric lathe in the workshop, in Hersbruck camp, as I will describe later in this book.

We did the Rentgen experiments and many more. I learnt how to make hair stand straight up, twice!

When our chemistry was well advanced, we used to play various tricks. When our much-loved professor would walk into the classroom, we would always stand and say either, 'Good morning' or 'Good afternoon'. All of a sudden he would be jumping up because we had spread crackling powder on the floor (like the kind used in pistol caps). It was very naughty, but he was a very good chap and we were forgiven.

The other tricks were done outside. We would make a tiny hole in the edge of a small coin and thin cotton would be threaded through it. It was then thrown over the telegraph wires on either side of the street and we waited for people to react upon seeing the small coin on the pavement. They would first look around, then quickly bend down to pick it up – but it would move – because we pulled the string! We had hours of fun. We had learnt that particular joke from the shop nearby. The owner stuck a ten-zloty coin to the floor, close to the counter – you should have seen the customers trying to get the coin!

The customers would drop gloves or hat in an attempt to get the coin; when they bent down to pick up these items again, they would see a notice on the vertical face of the counter: 'That's how our glue works.' The shop-keeper had to remove this coin though, because he was rapidly losing his customers!

At our home, which was by that time just beautifully completed, we worked hard in the garden. Our first two dogs had died of old age and we acquired two cocker spaniels. They were very good friends, but like all spaniels, lazy on long walks. They would just lie down on the footpath, waiting to be picked up and carried. Very sweet, but also a very heavy load.

My father was very good with wild animals and birds; once on a walk in the woods, he suddenly bent down and picked up a baby hare, just to show us; it was crying like a baby. Then it ran away, as fast as an arrow, into the forest. I used to walk with my father, in my young days, to pick mushrooms, proper ones, not like you buy today in the supermarket. My mother would make a tasty dish of them for our supper.

One of the spaniels, called *Ami* (meaning friend), would do anything I trained him to do. He would walk like an acrobat, along the four-inch beam used for beating the carpets... I loved my animals and my pets, and I miss them very much as they were always my friends.

During the winter holidays, we visited the Olympic stadium, including the slalom runs. This was a hair-raising experience. However, the daily trips to school and back again on skis were very enjoyable. This was our routine in wintertime and was very entertaining.

I remember very well our last winter holiday in the mountains. At first we stayed in the town Zakopane, but for the rest of our holiday we went to the highlanders' hut in the mountains. There were parties almost every other evening, on skis of course. We would visit the girls' camp, about two or three miles away.

For the slalom, which I have already mentioned, we had to go by funicular railway, to the 3,000-metre mountain top of Kasprowy Wierch. The slalom track was about 1,000 metres to the valley below. We were instructed to be very careful, (the slope was almost 70 °C to the vertical) and to go on our skis very slowly, horizontally, step by step. I was watching the Olympic riders, riding down in beautiful, rhythmic moves, and they were at the bottom in no time. Therefore, I decided to try this method myself. I was at the bottom of the slope in seconds, but most of the time I travelled on my tummy. Fortunately, apart from the shock, I had not injured myself, and what was most important, I had not broken the skis.

One of the most exciting rides down the mountains was along a bobsleigh track. Although hair-raising, it was a very enjoyable experience.

On the other hand, riding through the gentle mountain slopes was like a dream; we could ride more than twelve kilometres without stopping through the pine forest.

Then we would sunburn ourselves, lying bare to the waist on icy snow, on the south slope – it was beautiful and very warm.

On market day, we would take advantage by attaching our ski sticks to the peasants' sledges and have a free lift on the pathway to the school. Once, both Mietek and I got lost in our local forest mountains. We went round in circles for about four hours and it was only because we touched the trees to find the direction of north that we managed to get home. Our reception was rather a rough one.

One of my friends was a cinema maniac. There were three cinemas in Kielce, with two programmes per week in each of them. He not only saw all the performances, but he kept an exact record of actors, titles, locations, plus his opinion of the film on a scale from one to ten. We would always rely on this. (I met him in 1951 in England, when he was already working in the film industry.)

I was in charge of some youth organisations, and this also worked very well. There was colossal cooperation between all boys, to the extent that any obstinate individual would be severely punished, and he would not dare to complain to anyone from the teaching staff.

Once in our school, we had to create a model battle of great magnitude between the Poles and Russians (the old Russians). It was like Waterloo; the enormous field was made of plaster, with hills, trees and a river. Everyone had to contribute something. Soldiers on foot or on horseback, cannons, campsites, observation points. It was, as they say today, 'a big one'. The cannons were lifelike models, with little cartridges that would fire when lit by a match. The form was divided into offensive groups and the defenders. This was probably in the third or fourth form. My father used the fretsaw blade, after drawing the soldiers or horse riders. He would cut them out of plywood and my job was to paint them.

On the day, there were dozens and dozens of soldiers. The battlefield was about six foot square and the story was repeated exactly in our small way. There was great cannon firing, attack and surrender. Victory. I think I will remember it always.

I would now like to recollect some of the very pleasant social activities at my grammar school.

Our gymnasium occupied the whole of the top floor. It had great headroom, and was very well equipped; so much so, that beside PE, during the rainy days we could play basketball, volleyball, even five-a-side football. All around the room there were floor to ceiling ladders, dozens of full-length climbing ropes. There was provision for the easy erection of four-foot wide beams for acrobatics, vaulting horses, mattresses. Our physical education was at its best.

However, on special occasions our gym was transformed into a theatre, show-house, concert hall or even a ballroom.

The last one was of great importance, as near the end of the last year there was a graduation ball. It was a splendid occasion to show our school's abilities to the best and, of course, our individual talents. Each year the theme for the decoration was chosen by the top form boys. The committee would be formed and, with some financial help from the school, that theme would be developed. It was breathtaking for the younger students when they entered on the day of the ball. I must add that the theme and its interpretation were closely guarded secrets by the two top forms.

I remember that we had the 'Geisha' theme, which was of course a Japanese decor. One year there had been a Viennese theme; there were historical themes, and even a modern jazz theme.

All the walls would be panelled in plywood or thick boards; an artificial ceiling would be suspended above with large decorative lampshades. I remember once, we had blue netting for the sky, with stars, moon and even a comet. The walls would be painted with the appropriate scenes. In the Viennese theme there were short cross walls, forming individual niches, with tables for two. The parquet floor would be extra well polished. All the windows were blocked – the lighting effect was artificial only.

The number of boys would be counted and passed to the head boy, who in turn would pass it to the director. He would then apply to all three girls' grammar schools, for the corresponding number of girls. I do not remember which year was the lowest, when one would be allowed to participate, all I remember is that only the top form boys and girls could invite their personal friends, and would not be dressed in school uniform. All the other pupils would have to wear their school uniform. Every boy would have to have a white handkerchief during the dance. The orchestra was our own – and very good. On the day we would line the large stairs, bottom to top, awaiting the girls (also in school uniform; black skirts and white blouses – except for the top form). When they would arrive they would climb the stairs, and the head boy would introduce every girl to all of us. It was very emotional! At the start the director and his wife, and some of the staff, would take the floor for the first dance with some girls. Then they would disappear to the floor below, where an improvised kitchen, for cold drinks and snacks, was arranged. The staff would not interfere during the ball, but the head boy would be responsible for the order, and would see that no boy or girl would be 'supporting the walls'. No chance of that! The ball would last about three hours, and then the girls would be escorted by their parents, who would arrive at a set time and wait in the vestibule. Everything would then be finished until the next year. Of course, the next day, which was normally Sunday, after church, the whole place would be stripped so that on Monday it could be used again for PE.

There were, of course, talks, gossiping and spying, about who favoured whom, and so on. However, everything was in the best spirit.

As I am talking about entertainment, I must add that at least once a year, there was a theatre play. It was not held in the school but at our theatre in Kielce, which was a large and very modern building.

Again, the play would be chosen by the boys (perhaps with some prompting by the director or the staff). This is where I learnt to produce good class scenery. The last play I remember was *Galazka Rozmarynu* (The Branch of Rosemary), by the famous Polish writer, Zygmunt Nowakowski. It was a colossal effort; the play was very patriotic and had several scenes set on the battlefield. We invited Mr Nowakowski, and he came to the performance. He was so impressed, that our school was in the daily papers. This boosted our morale enormously.

I remember designing a special machine with which the explosions from rifles and guns were shown on the battlefield, painted on the backcloth. The whole thing was so impressive that we had to give a second performance.

To return to my home life…

I was taught to play chess by my father, who was quite

good at it. Then I played a lot at school. Soon my father, who often played chess for money (small stakes), realised that I was getting not only better, but so good that I could beat him. I can understand it today, but when I was twelve to fourteen years old, it was difficult for me to understand why he was so agitated, why he was so keen to prove to me that I had already touched a piece, etc. I became angry and, as a result, all chessmen would find their place on the floor. Obviously, I had to be sorry. These days I certainly consider it as a training of my character.

My father was always very good about organising his business problems. This obviously reflected itself in organising work at home as well, especially the garden. 'Witold, let's go to the garden, to prepare new beds.'

I knew what that meant! My father would direct operations, and Witold, would be digging, raking, putting manure down, etc. This again, I now consider was good training for my patience, experience and obedience. I liked my father.

Later, when I was in the concentration camp, when the first parcel arrived from home, I recognised my father's care in preparing that parcel; it was perfect and everybody envied that.

My father loved me very much – I know that. However unkind he might have been to his wife or me, he always meant well. I am very sorry that he died at the age of forty-six years, but at least he knew that I went through the concentration camp alive.

His grave is in Kielce – with no one to look after it. That's why I would prefer to be cremated.

I missed many accounts of my life in Poland before the war. But there were one or two that have reflected on my later years, and to some extent, had the war not started in 1939, my life could have been dramatically different.

When I was in my first or second year of my grammar school, my father took me to a music teacher, who was to test my musical talents. It was an ordinary violin; I remember it as if it were today. I was given a violin, which I had never held in my hands before. The teacher, who was a concert performer, told me how to hold the instrument, and he then proceeded to play a simple tune on the piano, which he asked me to repeat on the violin. To the great astonishment of my father and the teacher, I played exactly the same tune on the violin. I had several lessons to teach me the basic principle of that instrument, which took most of the two terms. When my school-teacher discovered my new talent he immediately enrolled me into the school orchestra, in the second violin section. It was simply a disaster! I could not follow anything – therefore, to save face, I was moving the bow over the strings so that it would not touch them. I observed the direction of the movement of the bow, up and down. Obviously, this could not last long and I was soon discovered!

As I was already in the school choir, the teacher said, 'We have to try to experiment two things with you: a) solo singing and b) some brass instrument.' As I was a big, strong boy, the brass instrument was a bass tuba, and as with the violin, I was asked to play a simple tune – which I did! But this time, not being impressed with the instrument, I began playing tricks, which the professor took as my inability to cope with this kind of music.

It was then that I was given by my uncle from south-west Poland – who was from a very wealthy family – a beautiful cello. The cello was not full size but three-quarter size. It was a very old instrument, built in Czechoslovakia, in Stradivari's time. I simply fell in love with this instrument and had many lessons to learn how to play it. I played both solo and in the school orchestra, and if the war had not begun, I would be a very competent cello player; not perhaps as good as Paul Tortelier or Jacqueline Du Pré, but certainly a very good one. I loved that cello very much indeed. Incidentally, my uncle played for many years in a famous Polish quartet.

My mother, before coming to England, had to sell this cello – a sad story.

Meanwhile, my voice was being trained very regularly by my teacher, for both solo and chorus singing. I remember that in 1938 our school choir won the second prize, out of twenty or thirty schools. Later I joined the cathedral choir, and sang proudly the Hallelujah Chorus from Handel's *Messiah*.

Besides normal education, which was wide indeed, once a fortnight we attended two periods of practical and tactical cadet force; this was from the fourth form onwards. This included: shooting range, camps, arduous walks, recognition of planes (ours and foreign ones), canoeing and various other sports, outside the school curriculum.

Every year we would go for a week-long camp, and in the matriculation year, we would go for four weeks. This camp included proper war activities, with shooting from rifles or machine guns (using blanks, of course). Such camps would include up to ten grammar schools. Training was very tough, conducted by both professional and reserve officers, and other ranks. It did not matter that some regular officers, not to mention other ranks, were well below our standard. They knew their job well and they did their best.

The school would subsidise the scout camps and our scout movement in general. Our equipment consisted of ten large tents, one dining tent, one for the toilets, and one for the kitchen. The quartermaster's job was extremely important: to provide enough plates and cutlery for all; then to choose a cook and helpers' jobs, which were taken tent by tent, in rotation.

Usually, in the first week, there were some complaints about the culinary work, but later on the filling of everyone's tummies prevailed and complaints ceased. Two parcels were allowed to be sent by the parents over the duration of the camp. The other problem was connected with the night alarms, when the whole camp would have to be packed up, except for the tents, and we would have exercise in the form of a three or four mile walk at 2 a.m. (for many, a great experience). There was always an armed night watch at the camp.

Once this proved to be a godsend to us; we were in a mountainous area, when a small river swelled until it was two miles wide, into an almost continuous lake. We had been woken up around midnight for a full alarm and were not allowed to come out of our tents. Water was already around the camp area, so, tent by tent, we scrambled to safety – to a farmhouse on the adjoining mountain. We saw houses with people and animals floating on them. Even a big bridge collapsed on our side.

Food had to be dropped by plane for us. We stayed like that for two weeks, completely isolated from the rest of the world. Everyone survived, and the traditional top of the camp mast was cut to be put in our headquarters cupboard, signed by every member as usual. The worst part of the exercise was, after coming back home and starting school, the first essay we had to write was to describe our experiences!

The last scouting camp before the war was in the extreme north-east of Poland, on the banks of the huge Lake Drywiaty. The whole organisation of the camp was put in my hands. I was sent to choose a site much nearer, but I did not like it. The first site was some 400 kilometres from Kielce. However, I preferred another site, which was recommended to me by the local people in Wilno. Unfortunately, I had an extra 250 kilometres to travel to this place, which would make a terrible difference, as I found out. The last one hundred kilometres was travelled in a narrow-gauge train with only two carriages. You have to remember that I was only eighteen years old, and when I was told there was also a training area for the Olympic swimmers and canoeists, the site was certainly approved.

I feel that I have to say more about the choice for this last camp. I was given instructions, money and an introduction from our school's director. First I went to Wilno, (now under the Lithuanians). One of my father's relations lived there; he was an officer in the Polish army. I went to see him, explained my mission, and his immediate advice to me was to go further north.

The countryside was very beautiful, but I was coming close to the north-eastern border with Russia. This was very difficult, but who would think about it then?

I stepped out of the train and walked towards the lake – it was like a dream. Unfortunately, I didn't know anyone in the area; therefore, with the night approaching, I slept rough on the banks of the lake.

In the morning, after smartening myself up, I went to

the town hall. I was received by the mayor, and in his Buick, I was driven around the lake to look for a suitable site. I was very grateful for his help and we eventually found a beautiful place.

On the way back to Kielce, I had to stop in Warsaw to book the site with its owners (the Central Institute of Physical Education). This I did, and then boarded the next train to Kielce. I was already preparing myself to face a limited time left for going to the cadet officer training camp, because I had overstayed my time my allocated searching period to find the camping site for my scouts. This camp was located in south-east Poland.

The captain for the first two weeks of the scouting camp was my deputy, Komeda (the camp lasted four weeks). Between 10 and 11 p.m., armed with full maps and a description of the site, I passed all the necessary information to Komeda. My cadet army rucksack, rifle and complete army uniform, was prepared by my mother. At 4 a.m. the following morning, I was on my way with other cadets, in the special lorries, to the south of Poland, where about 1,000 cadets had their camp.

Unfortunately, on the first day, as it was glorious summer, I spent the whole day playing volleyball with no shirt. As a result, for the rest of the camp time (fourteen days), I was excused from all exercises, especially carrying the rifle. Apparently, the first aid army doctor had never seen such blisters as I had on my arms and back. This was to my liking, as I was really tired by that time. The only thing that I did not escape was the early morning army exercise, with full uniform and equipment, running for about fourteen kilometres each way. On the way back, we had to carry some of our colleagues, for whom such a march was physically not possible.

On my return to Kielce, I had, again, one day to go to Drywiaty, to lead the remaining two weeks of our scouting camp.

The journey, however long (600 kilometres), was uneventful. On my arrival I could not find the camp. My original instructions to Komeda had obviously been misunderstood, and they have chosen a different site.

I eventually found them – it was not too bad. One good thing, which I found out later, was that not far away there was a Girl Guide camp from Warsaw, whose commandant, Jola, was to become my future wife.

From that time on, we had a very happy fourteen days, combining our exercises, creating the happiest memories for the rest of our lives.

It has to be remembered that the Girl Guides had a working camp on the Russian border, where most of the people were illiterate, but influenced already by Russian communism. Their work was very hard, even with the help of the Polish border guard.

On the way home we stopped for a day in Warsaw, and I was invited to Jola's home. It was a very memorable day (her mother was on their camp too, as parental help), except for the dog, who frightened me very much, as it was very dangerous – it was a Dobermann.

We parted, promising further contact, though not knowing what the future would bring (the war!).

One thing I must add is that at that last camp, before the war, I made many friends in the Girl Guide camp besides Jola. Those friends were very dear to me during the war days, and during my life in England. We, Jola and I, and lately, Maxine and I, visited Warsaw, and they visited us in London. It is a friendship that lasts to the very end and I am very grateful for that privilege.

To conclude this first chapter, it would be very appropriate to dwell a little on the subject of scouting.

I consider, that beside religious, theoretical, practical and social education, scouting contributed mostly to the development of my personality, to make me very responsible. For judging other people and their deeds, for curbing my 'wants' and 'desires', even if sometimes it meant losing a bit of my pride.

Scout training helped me to struggle through the early stages of war, through my very hard college days, through my first practice and through the concentration camp. In fact, without that scout training, I don't think I could have faced all the trials of my long life. If I received any scars, they are the results of mental injuries caused mainly by other people, especially by their attitude to life, their cruelty, or their arrogance, and lastly by their giving in to the temptations of life.

Due to my scouting years, I learnt to appreciate my talents, given to me by providence.

I am mostly proud of the fact that, during the whole of my scouting life, after the older ones first trained me, then in turn I was the one who trained others. However, the principles, based on the original idea of the whole movement, conceived by Baden-Powell (with only very small adjustments) were maintained to the full. The proof of this is the fact that so many of my friends from the scouting days maintained their contact over so many years and, when comparing our notes, I found how similarly their lives were cultivated, so that the very principle I just mentioned, was fully maintained.

I was lucky to meet my first wife, Jola, at that camp in the north-east of Poland. Through her I made good, solid contacts, with many of her Girl Guide friends, which lasted well beyond her shortened life. The memory of that camp has been well imprinted in my mind, together with the happiness and knowledge that one can stick to one's well-learnt principles.

Still in Poland, but under Occupation

The school diploma coincided almost with the war being declared by Germany. I, together with the whole company of the cadet force, was assigned to the job of liaison officer, linking the whole country. It was my first experience:

a) to receive the first telephone call from the Polish Railway Station tunnel near Cracow, which was a two-kilometre tunnel. The German planes were apparently wearing Polish markings when they dropped their first bombs. I had to inform five centres in the whole of Poland, by a special line.

b) to join the reserve officers in obtaining food, horses, men, etc. for the war service.

c) to organise the first camp of about 400 refugees, already fleeing from the West and the Germans. These refugees were provided with one of the biggest halls in Kielce. One of the families, under my care, consisted of nineteen people. There had actually been twenty-one people, but the father and oldest son were fighting in the war (the mother was only forty-six years old). They helped each other quite a lot and I had few problems to solve. Unfortunately, my duty there did not last longer than ten days, when everyone had to take care of themselves and depart to the East. I remember how in the army headquarters, we had been removing magazines and dismantling the rifles, before saying goodbye to each other.

This story of the beginning of the Second World War requires fuller explanation, if only for one reason – that the whole of my future life, including my presence in Ixworth, was prepared and organised for me there and then, perhaps by providence.

As I said at the beginning of this chapter, the war started on 1 September 1939. However, a few months earlier, there were already rumours of some activity on the political front. There was a meeting between our Foreign Minister and his German counterpart. Everybody, except for the British Government (who refused to see the reality), knew that Hitler was preparing his people, including the whole German army, for a confrontation. Austria, Hitler's birthplace, was the first sign. There was Czechoslovakia, in 1939, and so on and so on. We also knew that the great *Duce*, Mussolini, was preparing Italy with similar ideas, after capturing Abyssinia in 1936 and Ethiopia. These facts were recognised by Britain. So, just before the start of the war, about one month earlier, our forces had been put on alert. First, there was partial, and then full mobilisation.

I was in the cadet force and was fully mobilised. The telephone lines were laid so that my town, being in the centre of Poland, would be directly linked with five Polish centres: Warsaw, Lwow, Cracow, Gdansk and Wilno. Simply by pressing a button I could speak to all of them. The messages would then be relayed to the various headquarters.

But before that, there were preparations in earnest for the eventuality of war. Some of my friends, like myself, were permanently stationed at the telephone exchange centre. Some of my friends were stationed with the nuns, at a nunnery two miles from Kielce in Karczowka. (Incidentally, this was the place where my mother had started her teaching career.) The boys in that nunnery had a grand time, to the dismay of the Mother Superior. They were there for special training.

We had been given mobilisation orders about one week before the actual war started. It meant that I, along with some of my friends and several reserve officers, would be called to the commander-in-chief's office, and he would open, in our presence, the mobilisation papers. For the next two days and nights, we were travelling from house to house, farm to farm, workshops and factories, to hand over the papers and demand under order – with the threat of arrest or even shooting if necessary – horses, carts, cars, food, blankets, bedding, etc. These mobilisation papers were written out many years earlier and because of this it was sometimes difficult to trace any firms or individuals, as they no longer existed, or had moved away. Anyway, that was my 'christening' of war fever.

Back at my post at the telephone exchange, the first message on the night before the war was that a storm had damaged fuses on one mast of the high tension cable line. A few of my colleagues went to that place; they had only a very vague idea of what to do, but with the help of an electrician, they climbed the post (in pouring rain, and gale-force winds) and with special long tongs, successfully exchanged the burnt-out fuses for new ones. It was very brave of them!

Meanwhile, at about 4 a.m. the next morning, I received a call from the Polish town tunnel (it was actually a long railway tunnel) that it had been bombed by German planes with Polish markings on their wings.

You can imagine my excitement. I was the first to press the button, to tell everyone of the invasion. 'Hallo, Warsaw, Cracow,' and so on. Unfortunately, my elation did not last more than twelve hours. The crossing of the Polish border by German tanks was almost immediately confirmed, and the war of confronting the 'German Might' started in earnest. The strength of that army, and its speed, was unbelievable.

The first problem was that of the evacuees, running away from the German army. It was known from our history how brutal German soldiers could be.

As I said earlier, I was put in charge of 400 refugees. It was a mammoth operation, and again I can say that thanks to my training, both grammar school and scouting, I could manage to organise this camp, and run it for the first week or so. Soon after I was called back to my post at the telephone exchange and told by the commanding officer, 'You are all now released of your obligations to serve the country, and you have to care for yourselves, as from now on.'

This was a blow – a terrible blow. I looked round and I saw the other soldiers and cadets dismantling rifles, putting rifles in one room, magazines in another, and ammunition in the third room. Even with my lack of experience, it was ludicrous! It indicated the general collapse of both incentive to fight and morale.

I went out to go home. On the way, close to home, I met my father and mother, who were proceeding to meet me; they were holding my rucksack, fully packed, and some money. They told me that I must go away, as quickly as possible; they begged me to go east, to meet some of my mother's relations. What a send-off!

There is one very poignant epitaph to this. My mother handed me a note. It was from Jola. She was returning from the south, where she had been on a special sanitary course, when the train had stopped in Kielce. She had written the little note to me, and had asked a young boy whom she saw on the platform, whether he knew 'Witold'.

'Yes,' the youth replied. 'He is our scout master.'

'Could you deliver this note to him?' Jola asked. 'Of course,' was the reply. The note was delivered, the same day, to my mother. You can make your own deductions from this...

So, I started my journey. When walking through the high street I saw young people breaking shop windows, taking whatever they could – complete insanity.

I watched a column of soldiers returning from the West. When I asked where they were heading, the reply was, 'Radom and Warsaw.' So I joined them. I sat on one of the carts and fell asleep. I must have been completely exhausted, because when I woke up, we were nearing Warsaw, a distance of about 300 kilometres. They gave me a bike, and I said goodbye, and thanked them. I decided to head towards Warsaw.

With some luck, a convoy of about four army trucks, seeing a solitary soldier in cadet officer uniform on a bike, stopped and asked me where I was going. I replied, 'I don't know, perhaps east.' They told me to get on the lorry, as they were delivering supplies to the northern front, so they could give me a lift to Brest, on the River Bug, a further 200 kilometres away.

So I went, not even seeing Warsaw.

On the first stop we got some small loaves of bread,

and on the second stop at a monastery we saw how the cheese was made (similar to Edam). These monks had been famous for making that particular cheese for many years. In the cellars, we saw rows and rows of cheeses, each batch marked with its age. We eventually arrived at the right age group and the cheeses were loaded on to the lorry. We departed and a little further on at a crossroads; they bluntly told me that this was as far as they would take me. However much I wanted, they refused to take me any further. They gave me one whole cheese and two loaves of bread, and told me to go to the station of Brzesc, and to board the train to Rzeszow. Rzeszow, was much further south. They went north. I wonder what happened to the captain and his men. I should be thankful to them – or should I?

If I had known what I would be faced with, most probably I would have returned to Kielce, or gone to Warsaw. However, in the event, I decided to walk to the town and go to the station.

I took a train to a place somewhere in the middle of Poland (Rzeszow). Unfortunately the train stopped at Chelm and we were made to disembark, and told to make our own way. There was the River Bug, which was very wide. I, along with a few other people, negotiated with the local fisherman to take us across this river at night. The reason for this conspiracy was that the Polish Government, in their wisdom, decided that people should stop fleeing to the East. The Vistula and Bug rivers would be the borderline. Under the threat of being shot by our own soldiers, we crossed the river.

Somehow, early in the morning, we found ourselves on the other bank.

We did not expect an immediate welcome, but we also

did not expect German fighter planes. What saved us, or at least me, were the concrete rings, left on the field in preparation for the construction of a well. I simply crawled into one and played hide-and-seek with the German pilots. There were several planes and they made many circles, shooting at people. After the planes had finally gone, I went on foot to Kowel (a distance of one hundred kilometres). I did that journey in one very long day. I then decided that, seeing hundreds of Polish soldiers not knowing what to do, that I had enough, and I was going to return home. So I walked the same one hundred kilometres back, in a slightly longer time.

Chelm is in a valley, by the River Bug (which I had crossed earlier). When I arrived on a hill overlooking Chelm, I realised that the whole town was ablaze. Why I did the following, I do not know – I was obviously confused as to the best course of action to take. Therefore, I walked back a third time. On the way back, about halfway, I met an Austrian Jewish doctor. He could hardly speak Polish, but we understood each other in German. He had just completed his education, and he asked, 'Can I join you?'

'Of course,' was my answer, but after some hours of walking, night came and we had to rest somewhere. It was Saturday – the Jewish Sabbath. He asked me to wait for ten minutes, so that he could arrange a place for us to stay. That particular village was 90 per cent Jewish.

He returned and said, 'We will have a proper Jewish Sabbath and a good night's sleep.'

'But I do not know Jewish, nor their customs,' I said.

'Don't worry, I don't speak Yiddish either, but if you speak one-third Polish, one-third German, and one-third Yiddish of what you know, you will be all right,' he replied.

We arrived at a house. It was a small but very well kept, detached building. I was introduced to the family. They were all petrified, for the approach of the Germans, for any Jew, was like being condemned. I did not understand then – but I am fully aware of this fact today. The family were Orthodox Jews.

We were ushered to the first floor, where the rest of the family were already gathered around the table. The table had been very carefully decorated. There were many plates and little dishes with various sauces, spices, jams, herrings and things, which I had never seen before. There were small glasses for their special drink. Only the father, sons, and my companion and I were allowed to sit at the table. The wife and the two daughters would do all the serving and see that everyone was fully contented.

Before we were invited to eat, the father stood up and put on a Jewish cloak and shawl. On his forehead was strapped a phylactery, a well-constructed leather box containing the sacred words of Hebrew Scriptures. He began delivering a long sermon. The candles in the candlesticks were arranged in the traditional, arch-like, silver stand; they were lit and, after more prayers, we were invited to have a toast. Only then, were the wife and daughters seated at the table.

We spoke very little, as the atmosphere that evening was very sombre. We told them of the fire at Chelm, which made them very worried. Our story did not make the situation any easier. Later everyone went to bed, and we were given two straw mattresses in a small side room. In the morning the wife greeted us with a cup of tea – we washed ourselves and after a great 'thank you' we departed back to Kowel.

Just before reaching Kowel, my companion became

very ill with serious dysentery. Somehow, I managed to help him to the hospital. After making sure that he was in good hands, I bade him farewell, and went to the station.

I never expected what was awaiting me there. A German air raid again – this time they hit a standing train. Unfortunately, it was a munitions train. Part of it exploded. Shells, large and small, whizzed above my head. I sheltered under an old goods wagon and I waited like that for one, two, or three hours. Then I noticed that part of the train had departed – it was thanks to a very brave station guard, who was able to climb under the train and to unfasten the damaged part. I hope he received a medal for his bravery.

There was only one train on this station under steam and ready to go. Without knowing where I was going, I jumped into the nearest carriage.

It was a very long journey to Pinsk (near the eastern border), quite a large town of about 30,000 people. I was thankful for the cheese and bread, of which I still had some left.

On arrival, I went to the stationmaster to enquire about the situation. He replied, 'I am in the process of discussing on the telephone with the Russian Commander whether we will oppose their occupation of Pinsk.' I told him that there might be some local resistance. He said, 'We are still discussing it. Neither we nor they want any bloodshed.'

As it was already late at night, I departed to the town, and with some persuasion, and some money, I was given a small room in a very poor hotel.

The next morning, I went to the town again and I noticed that most of the houses were already decorated with red flags. The Polish flag is white at the top, and red at the bottom. What the people had been doing, was to tear away the white part, simply leaving the red flag.

I said to myself, 'There is no time to waste; I have to change my uniform into civilian clothes.' Again, with some forceful persuasion, I managed to get the civilian clothes, almost the right fit. When I was on the way to my hotel I had already heard shouts of jubilation and noises of the horse riders on the stony street. When I went to the cathedral square the situation was much worse. The cathedral square was next to the large River Pina; there was a link with the East via a large bridge across the river. That bridge had earlier been blown up by patriots. They had been misinformed, because the Russians, with their amphibious tanks, crossed the river and immediately started reprisals. They had been told that the Polish soldiers were hiding in the nearby church. The church was completely destroyed by small cannons. One of the shells hit the electric wire and it sprang along the whole perimeter of the square. The experience was simply terrifying.

I ran to my hotel, took my things, pinched a blanket and made my way to the station. To my relief there was the only train, about to go to Kowel. What irony! Unfortunately, the train was a goods train, with a majority of water tankers. The blanket helped – I fixed myself to the top access hole on one of the tankers, and I travelled like that for two nights and a day. This time the route of the train was very long and ran along the Russian border. It was really unbelievable to find oneself back where I had already been twice. This time, however, there were Russians in control.

On arrival, four Polish officers and I were arrested by Russian soldiers, and taken to their headquarters. I did not know any Russian; therefore, it was left to the officers to do the talking. After several hours, by some miracle, without a word of explanation, we were taken back to the station by the same Russian soldiers, with their bayonets fixed. There they saluted us and departed!

On the way to the station, we smelled freshly baked bread (it was 4 a.m.) and we asked the soldiers whether we could have some. 'Oh yes,' they replied, and they took us to the bakery. The baker, seeing Russian soldiers, with bayonets on their rifles, gave us the best possible bread and buns. Before departing, I noticed one thing that will always ring in my ears – there was a loud cricket in the bakery, which is a good omen.

One postscript to this story is that most probably one of my friends from Kielce was at Kowel station, and seeing my predicament, assumed that I was taken by Russian soldiers to Siberia. That was the message my mother received before my return.

However, in the end, I took the next train to Lwow, where I knew some well-off members of my mother's family were living.

It was a very uneventful journey to Lwow, a large university town. I had been there several times before; I even remembered where the second oldest member of my mother's family lived – Fredro Street. There I went. He was probably seventy years old; as a professor at the university he also held a high position in education circles, including that of the Ministry of Education. I understood that he often set exam papers for various universities in Poland.

He was a humanist. To me he was the most sought after member of my family. I hoped I would obtain the best and the latest information from him. When he saw me, he found in me the best help: his house had been partly damaged due to the war action, and his huge library was almost on the verge of collapse. I spent two days in his house, working like a horse, rarely finding a moment to eat and eventually to find out what I was actually doing in Lwow. That, I was told, is how the intellectual's mind works.

I remember his street name, Fredro, because that was once the name of a famous man, one of the best classical actors of satirical roles. This was also an 'ironic comedy'. I got from my uncle the address of the widow of his eldest brother, and there I went. My aunt knew very well how to manage in whatever difficult situation she found herself. Making some excuse to my uncle, I went to her house.

For the first time, I realised that I was completely lost in my life. It was late October. I had left Kielce on 9 September and I had had to rely entirely on my own wits.

The streets of Lwow were festooned with all sorts of decorations. On every corner were hanging huge loudspeakers announcing all kinds of information. The most important being, which was constantly repeated, that on 6 November, 'we' would be celebrating as every other year the famous Russian Revolution of 1917, and that Marshall Timoszenko would be on the platform to receive the parade. There were thousands upon thousands of Russian soldiers in Lwow.

Most of their rifles were hanging on strings because of the shortage of leather. Also, there was no difference between a marshall and a private, for in their army none of the coats, trousers, or jackets were hemmed. Therefore, they would not fit anyone; the only difference was the red metal insignia. One to five red triangles would indicate the lowest ranks. Similarly, one would grade the soldiers upwards by changing the shape from triangles to squares to rhomboids and eventually to stars. The marshall would have five stars.

I saw a huge crowd by one large Russian limousine. It was the car of Marshall Timoszenko, like the best Rolls Royce or Packard! The decorations along the main streets were vast. Before doing anything I found my Aunt Wanda. She lived in a large house, which could be regarded as a small-scale version of Harrods. My aunt's business was doing very well. She was very pleased to see me, allocated me a small spare room, gave me some clothes and told me to go to the Russian Office to be registered. She told me to come back quickly to her house as 'I have a lot of work for you'.

Again, no one asked me why I was there, almost as if they were fully informed. I found it very strange, and frankly disturbing.

It was not easy to register as there were hundreds of people like myself all trying to do the same. However, as soon as one of the officers realised that I had matriculated, and would like to study further, I became her friend. My prospects were fantastic. She was a Ukrainian girl and she advised me to go straight back to their college, and in 'two or three weeks', I would be fluent in Russian and of course Ukrainian.

I have to tell you a secret – the Russians conned the Ukrainians; they promised them independence and a great future too. (There are 33 million Ukrainians and they have never had their freedom even until now.)

It was unbelievable, but when the Germans, a couple of years later, overcame the Russians, they did exactly the same. They promised that the Ukrainians would have independence and freedom... The result in both cases was that the main sufferers were the Jewish people.

The proverbial pogrom occurred when the Russians came, and when the Germans conquered south-east Poland. Ukrainians never got their independence. I don't know how many people realise that the Ukrainian nation have their own social life, their own schools, colleges and universities. They have colossal national pride. Their folklore is probably one of the greatest in Eastern Europe. If you go through a Ukrainian village in the late evening, you will hear beautiful songs, sung by voices not trained, but natural – they are, in fact, even better than the Welsh. I know, I have heard them; I lived with them for one month.

I went to the college and learnt a lot of the Ukrainian language, and also learnt that, according to their teaching, their language was the mother of all East European languages. However, I came eventually to my officer friend and told her that I must go to Cracow, and from that moment our friendship ended. I got my papers and went back to my aunt, where, when I told her what I had done, she told me I was very stupid indeed!

Anyway, in the afternoon I was to collect, on the orders of my aunt, several boxes of sugar, butter and flour from the nearby mill. Each box weighed twenty-five kilograms, but the flour was in sacks of one hundred kilograms each. I had to carry these provisions to the second floor; I managed with one sack of flour, but the next one split on the top landing. (I was not prepared to compete with the strongman Geoff Capes!)

Perhaps my aunt was right, but I refused to be a slave to her idea of 'swimming on top of the very turbulent waters' and I refused to do all her donkey work for next to nothing.

There were three daughters there. The eldest was

Wanda, who was a dentist, whose husband was away at war. The next, Anka, was married on the day before the war began and, unfortunately, her husband was killed the day after. The youngest, Jasia, is still alive, and in a way was my favourite.

But contact was lost and only my mother sometimes exchanges letters with her.

I resented their mother's way of treating me, or anybody for that matter. It is very true that in those very difficult days for me, I fully earned my keep. It might not be very noble of me to say that, but it was true.

I got paid and looked for some other job. With sheer luck, I met another member of my family, Uncle Staszek. He suggested that we buy a horse and small cart, go to the railway yard, collect some coal, which was free, and sell it to the people in the town. It was another experience for me. He bargained for the horse and cart, and off we went to the station yard. We loaded the cart with coal, against strong opposition from similar enterprising individuals, and made our way to town. There was one snag – I did not tie the middle of the sideboards on the cart and we started losing some of our precious coal. To make things worse, we found that the width of the cart wheels were the same width as the tram rails – Lwow had a multitude of tram lines. You can imagine how behind us, the infuriated tram driver, made the ding, ding, ding noise, loud enough for everyone. My uncle and I were trying desperately to pick up the coal. I do not remember how this episode ended, but all I do know is that without the cart, horse and coal, my uncle and I ran away into the very large marketplace!

Somehow, we lost our pursuers and decided that the only way was to find the Pass Office, for our journey home. I don't remember what the money situation was, but somehow we managed. We were told by someone in the Pass Office (another young lady) that we were doing the wrong thing, and that she would arrange transport for us to Kiev and Moscow, especially after she heard that I had been training my voice.

She told me that 'artists' in Russia were treated as cultured people and always had a fantastic future. Eventually, we were given the promise that we would receive the passes within the two weeks. She was quite right about artists. All the artistically-minded people were paid extremely well – like Hollywood stars – when the rest of the population starved.

These were very busy weeks, especially as in between, was the prospect of that magnificent parade in Lwow, which I wanted to see, and in fact did witness. One little picture will give you an idea of the life then: in the morning it was rather rainy and the soldiers were wearing overcoats to go to the parade. However, nearing the parade time, the sun came out – no problem for the army. Soldiers approaching the parade ground would take off their coats and throw them on to a large heap. The heap of coats would be removed by a convoy of lorries. Soldiers, therefore, would go into the parade appropriately dressed – no overcoats.

I saw the 'top brass' without the brass, on a platform high in the air and thousands upon thousands of soldiers, men and women, guns, even aeroplanes. The parade lasted nearly four hours. It was extremely impressive, set against the decorations made of red flags arranged as huge flames. Plaster-made figures symbolising peace, learning, virtue and comradeship, were placed all over the parade ground.

A dozen or so planes flew above, and the whole ceremony was relayed through the loudspeakers on every street corner. As I said earlier, the very Polish town, Lwow, had three-quarters of a million people. It is also now in Russian hands. How sad!

We saw poor Russian soldiers with packs of completely worthless roubles, trying to buy anything which was new to them. They did not realise what bras were for, therefore, they used them as earmuffs. They used nightdresses as evening gowns – for men! They had never seen a wristwatch in their lives. Therefore, anything from an alarm clock to a compass would do, it would be strapped to the wrist. Things they would buy were beyond belief. I certainly would not believe, had I not seen it myself. Yet today, their watches are some of the best in the world, as are their cameras.

They were amused by ordinary zips or press studs – they considered them as toys. They were so naive that, in the marketplace, clever chaps would sell them pieces of potato wrapped in paper, as watches shown earlier. Screams and chases by the Russian soldiers would not produce any results.

Don't ask me how, but I found my uncle, and after collecting our passes and buying some food, we went to the station to travel to the temporary border between Russia and Germany. It was Przemysl, on the River San. The railway bridge was damaged; therefore we would have to be exchanged with the Poles from the West, crossing the wooden plank in the middle. This was not easy and we had to obtain new passes, which would give us new registration numbers, names of the whole family where we intended to go, etc. This took us three full days and nights. I even have a photograph, taken by an enterprising amateur, to record that moment.

This requires further explanation. By now, I think you must have some idea of the number of Poles who ran away from the invading Germans, hoping that somewhere in the East everything would be stopped, and by some miracle, a 'New Poland' would emerge. After all, the one hundred years of occupation had taught us many lessons. We went through three partitions and Poland emerged again. No one, even in his wildest dreams, thought that it could be as bad as we eventually discovered it to be – five years of the worst occupation that Poland had ever experienced.

But coming back to my story, the Russians would exchange with the Germans only a similar number of people going East or West. That was why we had to wait such a long time in order to get our passes. I know that even today, people will sleep on the pavement for two or even three nights to obtain a ticket for the 'Last Night of the Proms' at the Albert Hall, or to secure a place for the Harrods' sale, or even to watch the coronation or a royal wedding. But the people in those cases do it for pleasure; they are supplied with food and drink, they may even be photographed for television. In our case, we were hungry, we did not have adequate clothing and we did not know what we could expect tomorrow. We could, as so many before and after were, be taken by a lorry into the depths of Russia.

We were eventually led to that wooden plank, to be picked up by smart German soldiers, who kindly helped the old and disabled, as it was very slippery. On the German side, we were packed into cattle trains, rather roughly, fully locked and sealed, with bales of straw on the floor. Destination Cracow. Two days and nights we sat and slept, together. From time to time we were given some food and a chance to go out under escort. It was a very bizarre journey!

In Cracow, now in the middle of November, we disembarked and we were given a sort of passport known as a *Kenkarte*, this was to be used for the next four years. This held an instant photograph, and we would be considered 'free'. I boarded a train for Kielce immediately and at the end of November I was home again. A full three months – and so many events. I have told you only a very small part of them.

To return to my family. After a short rest my father assigned me to do a job, he was working again as an architect/engineer. I was put in charge of rebuilding several houses and barns in a neighbouring area of the Swietokrzyckie Mountains. This was a little above my abilities!

I located many of my school friends, we exchanged our stories and I found to my amazement how a lot of their experiences had not been too different from mine. Some held firmly to their principles, but others went very quickly astray. Some others disappeared into the woods to join the resistance movement.

In Kielce, I realised for the first time, how strong the anti-Semitic tendency was, boosted of course by German propaganda. One night we were woken by searchlights on the nearby open field, clearly visible from our windows. The Jews from day one, when the Germans invaded Poland, had had to wear the Star of David. We watched as they were led to that field. Later I was told that there were nearly 10,000 of them. The Jews had to dig a huge grave, then they approached the edge of that grave, took off all their clothes, and SS men machine-gunned them from guns mounted on the back of lorries. The bodies were then sprinkled with white powder, which must have contained phosphor. The next row followed, and so on, until the whole 10,000 were murdered. The clothes were searched, one by one, for jewellery and valuables, and the remains thrown on a heap and a fire would be lit to conceal their crime. That was my 'christening' as to what I would go through in the following years.

The German authorities believed that they were the only people, *herrenvolk*, suitable for education. As a result, any schools beyond primary, and a limited number of secondary, were forbidden for Poles. Universities were totally banned and only two so-called technical colleges were allowed. One was in Cracow, the other in Warsaw.

My father, in the course of his work, met a German by the name of Captain Hauptmann, who had lost his son, of exactly my age, on the first day of the war. When seeing me his eyes were full of tears. He was an ordinary soldier, hating all the SS. He promised my father that he would find a place for me in the technical college in Cracow. He kept his promise!

I remember going to the station in Kielce with my best friend Mietek. We had been talking and laughing whilst waiting for the train to Cracow.

There were SS soldiers walking along the platform and, for some reason, they thought I was laughing at them. I got a smack in the face and was commandeered to the office. There, I was fully interrogated, documents were examined and so on. I mentioned my father's *Wehrmacht* friend, Captain Hauptmann, and that did the trick. They almost immediately released me and I was still in time for my train. But I learnt my lesson. I can tell you that it was the only time in my whole life that I was struck across my face. Even in the concentration camp I was spared such humiliation – especially as it was delivered by a stupid private of the SS.

When I arrived in Cracow I went straight to my aunt's house. I was allocated a place to sleep. It was a camp bed, to be put out each night, and in the morning to be folded up and put away, all by me. That was the routine that I learnt during the next two years. The third year was much easier but that I will explain later.

The life with the Obermeyers (this was my uncle's family name), I remember having lots of pleasant moments. It was also full of routines, with many sorts of restrictive regulations, which were introduced to me during my stay there. On the other hand, the whole family were very kind and caring.

Fred Obermeyer was an elderly gentleman, who had lived his early life, in some comfort, in Austria's capital, Vienna. Cracow was still in the hands of the Austrian Empire. He joined the Austrian army, and was eventually discharged I think as either lieutenant or captain. He always remembered those days with great pleasure and excitement. It left him with traditional army obedience, strictness and a sense of duty.

His memories of happy Viennese life were always with him and you only had to start, 'How was it in the opera when the view of the stage was obstructed by the enormous hats of the ladies in front?', or any other subject of this sort – and soon the photographs would be produced, his face would brighten and only Auntie Hela could stop the monologue.

My auntie was a strict retired teacher and a hard-working housewife. She kept her eagle eye on the large tenement house they owned in Krowoderska Street.

They had one child, Zosia, who was my very good friend. She was some six years younger, but we enjoyed many happy moments full of games at home and in their very large garden. She would spend hours in the fruit trees, consuming the seemingly endless supply of pears or apples. She was an intelligent girl, but strictly looked after by her mother.

I will never forget the daily routine of grooming her hair. It was very long, probably more than a metre, and it was painstakingly combed by her mother, who would eventually make it into two lovely plaits.

The routine of my life with them, as I have already said, was very strict, but I got used to that and during my stay there it helped to curb my happy character, full of ideas for various innovations. On many occasions this was inspired by college friends and my past.

The daily routine in Krowoderska Street was not built on surprises. For instance, my uncle was chief cashier in one of the large banks in Cracow. There had to be two people in the bank at 8.45 a.m. every day, who could open the safe and distribute the money and securities to the clerks. Therefore, every morning my uncle would get up exactly at 7.30 a.m. and go to the bathroom, where unfortunately there was also the loo. In a sense it was a disaster, as he needed a minimum of three-quarters of an hour there; but we got used to this, and I would set my alarm half an hour earlier so that I could carry out my ablutions before he appeared. After a quick breakfast, he would depart to the bank, where, on the strike of 9 a.m., his cashier's window would open. I don't remember whether he was ever ill enough not to attend his duties.

For my Auntie Hela, the day began one hour earlier, having her washing and personal hygiene done before everyone else. She would prepare all breakfasts and wait for the various departures. There was also one elderly tenant, a friend of my uncle's, to be looked after. He died while I was there and I inherited his room for the last few months of my stay.

Her morning would be spent cleaning the house. Firstly, all windows would be opened so that the flat would be fully ventilated (summer or winter). Dusting, cleaning and polishing, especially the parquet floor, was a daily routine too.

There were also the weekly jobs, like my uncle's sharpening of his razor – it was sacrilege to interrupt this hourly performance. There was one animal in their house – a yapping dachshund, a complete nuisance; nobody was safe with this creature. I like nearly all animals – but this dog, however, was not my great friend, rather we tolerated each other. On the other hand, my uncle adored him. Auntie would not allow any feeding with scraps at the dinner table, (the parquet floor again), so my uncle secretly made himself a sort of stiff material pouch, which he would fix under his jacket, at the rear, just at belt level. His false teeth were not very good, so the harder pieces of meat would secretly find their way into the pouch, for the dog. Of course, everyone knew of this, but it would have been very unkind to dispel his illusions.

As I said earlier, their house was very large, with about a dozen tenants. There were three floors with an internal, continuous balcony overlooking the large square. It was a great tradition in Cracow that, from early morning, all different tradesmen would call to that yard loudly offering their services. There were pan and kettle repairers, glaziers and salesmen of various odds and ends. Very similar to Dickensian London.

All windows would have wooden shutters and the street lighting was still gas powered. Very early in the morning, a cart with coal would roll along the street, loud shouting would announce their presence and the price of a bag of coal. It was a very romantic time.

The daily polished parquet floor reminds me of an incident with my friends calling to see me. There were museum felt-type overshoes for them to wear inside the house! Tongue-in-cheek, they tolerated this requirement. Especially as one of my friends, Bohdan, had an eye for Zosia – but to no avail – everything was so strict and fully traditional, war or no war.

Otherwise, there were very few visitors coming to us. On the one hand it was good, but it is my feeling that it was unhealthy for Zosia, who spent most of her free time reading masses of books. The house, of course, was a mine of problems, which Auntie Hela would have to resolve for nearly every tenant. Leaking pipes, broken windows, draughts, unsafe balconies, and so on and so on. These problems occupied many hours daily, and we became fully acquainted with them. Zosia was obviously involved in those problems too, but being totally under the influence of her mother she quickly learned her future role of being in charge. She succeeded in performing all those duties well.

During my next few days I was enrolled at the technical college to study Civil and Structural Engineering. The syllabus was not up to university standard, therefore during that time I had additional coaching by the then completely unemployed university professors.

It was a very hard time, but very enjoyable too. Our group of students was very friendly – we all wanted to attain the best standards we could.

The professors were very good, especially the dean of the department. Professor Wierzchowski was fully devoted to his job. He knew very well that he was constantly under German surveillance; and he knew that the final exam would have to be in two languages, Polish and German, for our final diplomas.

I am very proud that I finished equal first with my friend Tombinski. I knew that I had learnt my trade well.

I used to go to extra lessons of higher maths with a university professor; his wife was also a mathematician in secondary education. He had an excellent method. For two hours I would sit in front of him, rapidly writing down whatever he would say. After that, I would have three days break, and then another two hour lesson, preceded by a quarter of an hour's questioning on the previous lesson. Eventually it worked and I became quite an expert on the subject.

On the lighter side, I remember one afternoon coming to their house, where my professor would be struggling to make the curtains work, when pulled to one end. It was simply beyond him. It took me ten minutes to solve the problem – he was simply amazed.

Our professors were from all walks of life. One teaching us architectural forms was an Egyptologist; thanks to him, I am an expert in this subject.

The one who taught us statistics was probably the best, but at one time he assumed that I was so good that he would check the other examination papers against mine. Unfortunately, after he had returned the papers, with only mine bearing a 100% mark, I went home and, after checking again, I found that I was wrong. On the next lesson, I went to him and told him that I had made a mistake. There was great pandemonium, but eventually he retrieved all the papers and returned them the following day – mine was not marked. We have been great friends since that time.

One subject which I valued almost as the best was Polish technical correspondences – it is a pity English students are not taught that subject at all. That was probably why I could manage so well in British offices, despite having such little knowledge of English.

We had, even under the watchful eyes of the Germans, a great time, including the final exams.

At this point I must mention something that was, and is even now, a greatly guarded pleasure of mine – music. As you know, from my early years I was trained, not only in playing various instruments but also in training my voice.

Due to some luck, I was introduced to Professor Jachimecki, who used to teach musicology at Jagiellonski University (which was not able to exist under the Germans). He took an immediate liking to me and I had free lessons with him twice a week. His wife was a French writer, but she knew Polish perfectly, so she helped in translating many classical items for my study of Polish language. He taught me how to breathe properly and how to express feelings so that listeners could be fully aware of what I was conveying to them. I was told I must sing in a way so that everyone could understand every single word. I wish people nowadays would do the same! My voice was a deep bass.

He took me to several private concerts and recitals. On one such occasion, I was introduced to a famous lady singer. She listened to my voice and when left alone she asked me straightforward questions:

a)   Have you – do you think – a good voice, and is your physique good?

b)   Are you prepared to abstain from the pleasures of life?

c)   Are you rich, or have you rich sponsors?

It was obvious that an affirmative could be given to the first question only. Nevertheless, I thanked her very much and she wished me luck.

I received my diploma on 18 June 1943. My music professor, learning that I intended to go to Warsaw, gave me an introduction letter to his friend – Mr Didur, the principal bass of the La Scala, Milan.

It was a great dilemma when I arrived in Warsaw – what to do? I met my future wife Jola again. Her father was the town planner and he had many contacts. At first he sent me to one building site of a big factory, of which, the top storey had been demolished by German bombs. I had to level the top concrete floor, to be ready for a flat timber roof. I was given a tiny level (very complicated) and a technical college student, to help me. This was on the eighth floor, with a huge cornice projecting along the whole perimeter. I was never afraid of heights, but my assistant was; that, perhaps, was my saving grace. I sent him for a coffee break, during which I quickly studied the instrument and my task fully. When he returned I was completely in control. He was amazed seeing me stand on the edge of the cornice stone – but the job was done in one day.

I was then persuaded by Jola's father to join the engineering firm of Oppmann and Kozlowski, who had just been given a large contract in eastern Poland. The contract was to rebuild the station workshops and to construct long ramps to receive Russian trains (wider rail gauge), at higher level, to be able to discharge their cargo directly to the European-type train below.

The place was called Malaszewicze, and I worked there for eighteen months, with two days holiday only. There were twelve engineers and 4,000 workmen. We were all housed in specially-built barracks. It was a mammoth operation, considering that the main line was in constant use, transporting troops to the East. At first, the 'goodies' the Germans collected in the East were sent on this railway line to the Fatherland.

We worked extremely hard, getting up at five or six in the morning and finishing well beyond lighting-up time in our offices. But it was always done with great camaraderie, throughout.

On my arrival, I was allocated my bed – there were probably six in the room – and then I was called to supper. After supper, I was asked whether I played bridge. I replied in the affirmative, so there were about four tables, and we played until about 10 p.m. Then it was time for a quick game of poker. It was really great fun – there was one player who could not keep secret what cards he had; he was always losing. But it was not about the money; it was pride. When we departed to our beds, I wished everyone goodnight. Because of the way my companions observed me, I felt suspicious. But in the morning, when I was asked how I slept – 'All right,' was my reply – then I looked at the sheets, they were full of blots of blood. Only then did I realise there were bedbugs. I also realised that the other beds, which were all of steel-frame construction, had the feet stuck in open cans of paraffin.

That was the end of the joke. I had the better of them though. Not only did I put paraffin cans under each leg of my bed, but I managed to get double-sided sticking tape, which I fixed on the ceiling, to cover the perimeter of my bed. This prevented the parachuting bedbugs from dropping on me. I was laughing the following morning. Eventually they discovered my method and everybody used it.

The other problem was rats. Every night we could hear the tip toes of rats running in the loft, there and back. If one left any food it would be gone by morning. Even food suspended in a net from the ceiling would be gone. The rats would climb the wall, and jump at the net.

We had at least ten or twenty traps for the rats, but that was not sufficient. All the barracks would be fumigated every month and then we would be free from those creatures for not more than a week.

I saw for the first time in my life how caught rats were killed. The trap would be taken to a field, and opened. The young, experienced boys would wait for the rat to run out of the trap and away. Then, because of the psychology of a rat, seeing the open space, he would run back to the trap and at that moment he would be clubbed to death.

It was a losing battle, because there were so many rats and mice, and they were constantly multiplying. That was why the general fumigation was a much more efficient way of getting rid of most of the vermin.

In our barracks, during the long winter we had wood- or coal-burning stoves, free-standing with the flue passing straight through the ceiling and roof.

When the fully-loaded German trains, with sunflower seeds, were standing on the sidings, we would go along the train, unwire the door and slide it open slightly. The seeds would seep out slowly and we would collect basketfuls and take them to the barracks. A large steel tray would be placed on the top of the stove with the seeds spread on it, to dry out nicely – soon ready to eat. We simply became addicted to those seeds. We became such experts, that we could put a dozen in the mouth and manipulate our tongues so that each seed would be shelled separately, and a dozen shells would finally be spat out. All the while the door of the railway wagon was left open and by morning all the seeds were on the ground. We were the 'little saboteurs'.

Our main job was the construction of the new concrete ramp, equal in length to the full length of the goods train. The Russian trains had wider gauge rails. Perhaps it was the decision of Tsar Nicholas I to make the Trans-Siberian Railway Line by putting a ruler on the map between Vladivostock and Moscow, and drawing a straight line. However difficult it was to construct it, it had to be built. Presumably the width of the track had something to do with it. The trains are wider and one and a half storey high, or one storey high for important dignitaries. It took, at one time, fourteen days on this journey, with the climate changing drastically. The travellers were fully equipped, with portable stoves and provisions necessary for such a long journey (I think the Canadian railway, also of normal gauge, was built in a similar way, and both are equally famous today). Nevertheless, the purpose of this story is to point out that a lot of very important people had curious ideas, because at the time they had the power to do it! Otherwise there would not have been the Seven Wonders of the World.

Let's come back to the ramp. The idea was very simple. The Germans wanted, very quickly, to transfer (free of charge) Russian grain and sunflower seeds, for oil - tons and tons of it. It was very easy to transfer from the Russian-style train above to the train below, by constructing simple chutes for such an operation. However, it was not long before we were given another task – to demolish the ramp, when the Germans started to lose the war with Russia on the Eastern front. That is why this operation was so important and we had to find experts to demolish such a quantity of reinforced solid concrete. We actually employed men from the nearby quarry who, however bewildered, won the contract very easily against tough competition. We did not have the pneumatic hammers at our disposal – it was 1943!

However, everyone was happy, and in eighteen months, I returned to Warsaw with more 'experience', knowing many Ukrainian songs from a lovely girl from the next village. This girl, because she did not listen to my advice, travelled a day earlier from Warsaw back home and was involved in a very serious rail accident, through the sabotage of the Underground Army. She was the only person who was thrown out of the train, partly scalping her head. I visited her the following day and she was recovering quite well.

She and her two small sons (her husband had been killed at the beginning of the war) were the only people I really admired during my eighteen months of isolation, because of their determination to live.

I used to visit their house about every other week. It was a great experience, as the village was probably five miles away. We knew nearly all the train drivers and, should I want to go to the village and 'thumb a lift', they would slow the train sufficiently for me to jump on the engine footplate. I would have a little talk with the driver and, five miles later, he would slow the train again and I would jump off. It was the same in the evening or morning, on the way back. It was much more difficult in the winter, but somehow we managed. I even remember having a drink of vodka on New Year's Eve with the driver. All the drivers were very good people.

Once while constructing a large inspection pit, when the concreting was already completed, but not fully cured, the driver of a 120-ton engine, wanted, sadly, to make a three-point turn as soon as possible. Yes, he reversed it – into the pit. Only with the help of the huge railway crane did we manage to lift it out, then repaired the wall and the engine, all within twenty-four hours.

The last weeks in Malaszewicze were like a nightmare because the remains of the German army, after being defeated by the Russians, were brought back with their dead and wounded. It was simply unbelievable that a million soldiers would return in such a condition. That was the beginning of my realisation of what I would see and experience before the Second World War ended.

The First World War was the simple killing of other soldiers – but the Second World War was very refined in its methods, which were simply beyond belief. This was equally applied in all nations from European to the far eastern Japanese.

To me it was another Gehenna, but perhaps we were a little better equipped and resilient. I reappeared in Warsaw. I met Jola again, who was by this time fully engaged in politics, so much so, that she had to simulate insanity and had been moved out of Warsaw by her father; otherwise her life would have been in danger from fellow Polish patriots of different political beliefs.

I must add here that Poland was already divided into many political factions, very often fighting against each other; some believing in the West, some in the East, and there were many 'don't knows'. One would have to be very careful what one would say, and to whom, before disclosing one's allegiance. Unfortunately, there were too many guns freely available and too many gun-happy owners. It was one of the reasons why the Russian army would not cross the Vistula River to help the Polish resistance fighters – simply barbaric.

By some peculiar contacts, not known to me at all, my father got linked with some Ukrainian organisation at a very high level. I was once invited to a Ukrainian high society dinner, where for the first time in my life I saw many counts, princesses, and so on, along with their very expensive jewellery.

Also, at the same time, I was co-opted to help to clear the Jewish ghetto, which by that time, after the famous fire, was fully and completely burnt out. There were, however, many building structures in a very dangerous condition (some up to nine storeys high and brick built). There were many and various pockets of Jews of the passive resistance movements, still having dreams of escaping into the West because of their connections, and their apparent wealth. They built very deep bunkers, stocked with food and all other necessities, even air-conditioning. All was prepared for the long siege.

Unfortunately, the Germans were armed with grenades and gas bombs, which they dropped liberally into those bunkers, killing the Jewish people like flies.

However, I know many Jews escaped to the West, especially their rabbis, along with other religious leaders. They often bravely risked their lives to fight for their principles against German might.

There was a story that a Swiss train would be waiting for them at the Swiss border and the Jews paid colossal ransom money in the hope of escape. They were all denounced and killed before ever reaching the Swiss border.

There is one story which I must convey to the readers – not because I want to be praised for it, but because it was a reflection of general feelings in most of the Polish citizens, to help the others – without expecting a reward.

I and a school friend called Bitny-Szlachto, after working in the ghetto, found out that a small group of influential Jews needed to be got out. We devised a method; on one of the large lorry carrying bricks from the demolished buildings we would first place a large wooden box, without a bottom, and without one side. It was deep enough to allow a person to slide in. We bribed the driver of one lorry and, the day before, we brought into the ghetto this wooden contraption.

Amazingly, we were not questioned on the German post into the ghetto, as they knew us. Next day, the Jews (five of them) were told where to wait. The box was laid on the lorry and bricks were loaded on top. At the given signal, one side of the lorry was opened. The Jews ran quickly and were helped into the tiny space. The side of the lorry was lifted into position, the driver and I approached the gate out. I had with me a large bottle of quality vodka, which I left at the guardhouse, and they, unsuspecting, let us out.

It was the last time I was in the ghetto. Anyway, it was

only three days before the Warsaw Uprising. I feel personally very proud of this.

There were, of course, many stories connected with my work in the Jewish ghetto.

Once, I remember, returning after lunch, I could not find my men – however, after a good search, I found them at the bottom of one collapsed building. All of them were crouching around a large dense wire net, fixed around a large square wooden frame. Two men would shovel the rubble on to this net and the rest of the men would eagerly observe the contents left on the net.

'What are you looking for?' I asked. They showed me a gold chain and a gold coin, also the remains of a little personal safe.

'There must be more of it here,' they said. I told them that they had one more hour for their investigation, before they had go back to normal work. I do not know whether they found any more, but they were very satisfied on the way out.

There is another rather gruesome story. The men when leaving the ghetto after work, even being searched by the German soldiers, would be able to get things out. On one occasion, I was told that a new pair of leather riding boots were brought for sale with the dealers. It was all very cloak-and-dagger. The boots were sold, but moments later the buyer ran screaming – there were legs still in the boots!

There were accidents too. When a row of houses were pulled down, the party walls were left standing. There were four of them. Suddenly, from the wind, they fell on each other like a pack of cards, on to a cart, horse and its driver, who were buried alive.

It is appropriate to finish the story of this chapter of

being still in Poland, but under German occupation, with two remarks. If I remember, there was no mourning in Kielce, Cracow or Warsaw, when we were told that a German civilian, collaborator or soldier had been killed by the Polish underground movement.

I was in the Underground Army. I was in Warsaw, in the so-called 'Warning Squad'. We would be given the instruction to go to a place and tell the listed person that it is the last warning for him or her, to toe the line, to be an obedient Polish person, otherwise, the alternative would be death. We would list all their wrongdoings. We would normally be working on a four to five person basis, accompanied by a girl, who would have a gun in her handbag. We were unarmed. We would walk to the place, tell them who we were and read the statement. After warning them that they must not inform the police, we would depart. There were never problems. I think I carried such instructions about ten times.

The other point which I did not mention, was that the Jewish ghettos were not only in Warsaw. There were many others, in different towns. However, through the high wall surrounding it, people would be fed through the small holes, or helped to escape, like Mrs Bregman and her daughter, by Jola's father. They were kept at Jola's mother's house and narrowly escaped arrest many times by the Gestapo. It was a trying time for everybody.

Then came the Warsaw Uprising.

Warsaw Uprising, Concentration Camp and Freedom

In two days' time, the Warsaw Uprising started, a few days earlier than anticipated. I was isolated, as I was living next to the German HQ, in Filtrowa Street, and was unable to reach my underground unit. The block where I was living contained flats occupied by about 400 Polish families, mostly widows or wives of killed or imprisoned Polish officers. They were the victims of the 1939 action.

I thought it would be the safest place for me to wait for the command, for the uprising which we knew to be imminent.

There have been many books written about the Warsaw Uprising and it would be impertinent to add my account. However, I feel that I should add my personal observations and experiences of the first ten days, or until I was arrested by the SS.

The last three days, after freeing the Jews from the ghetto, I was sitting tight in my quarters, knowing that I would be searched for by the Gestapo.

I had very good friends in the flats of one of the blocks, on the second floor. They were mostly widows or single women, some with children, waiting for their husbands, officers who had been arrested at the beginning of the war, and who were patiently waiting in POW camps in Germany. They knew each other, worked very hard for their living to send parcels with food, etc. to their husbands and to educate their children, and many of them worked in the underground organisations. I felt, therefore, safe with them, and they knew me well too.

When the Warsaw Uprising started our quadrangle of buildings was immediately closed by the SS, as we were next door to their headquarters.

We could only look through the windows, or hear on the radio, official German bulletins. When looking through the windows on one side, we would have a panoramic view of the filters area (the equivalent of a sewer disposal plant, for nearly the whole of Warsaw). It was a vast area covered with grassed fields. All the cleaning machinery was underground and there was no smell.

The area adjoining was the first to be cleared of the insurgents, the Polish army. Most of them were in civilian clothing, with white and red armbands, often wearing Polish army caps. Later, when some of the German units were captured, their armour and uniforms would be confiscated and worn by our underground army.

Unfortunately, in that area, this was a very short story, as the Germans were quickly in control with their tanks destroying and burning all adjoining buildings. It was a heartbreaking experience. We saw fires day and night, and later planes, ruining and destroying most of that part of Warsaw; we did not know and we had no idea that an almost similar situation was all over Warsaw. Only some areas of the city were in a better position and would last the whole two months of hard fighting.

On the third day, we noticed a large complement of German SS sitting along our block on the other side of the street, on the edge of the grassed area. They certainly appeared to us to be very well-known Tartars, enrolled into German units. They were most dreaded, wild, almost in-human creatures. They, we knew, were waiting to take us. They reminded us of the Polish King Sobieski, who defeated the Turks in Vienna in 1683, and earlier at Lwow. The Tartars went into action on the tenth day; they crashed the gates and, after searching for all inhabitants, took us to the field. We were prepared, having packed all we could, and ready to go.

We were ushered, in a very unceremonious way, in a long column and directed to the very large square, about one mile away. This was the wholesale marketplace for vegetables, fruits and flowers, for most of Warsaw. It was called Zieleniak.

It was almost dark, and the houses and villas around us were fully ablaze. We saw many people totally engulfed by flames, running away from the houses. They were human lanterns, like during the burning of Rome by Nero. It was simply terrifying. The SS men would not even react to this terrible sight. We thought that killing the burning people would be more humane than letting them die slowly.

We entered Zieleniak, already in an awful state of fright; however, it was nothing compared with our experiences over the whole night on that square. We all sat along the perimeter walls, not realising that the SS soldiers (of Tartar origin) were looking for young wenches to rape and kill. These we protected under our coats and only witnessed the carnage by the oppressors. I don't know how we managed to protect some of the young women from those beasts, but I saw many of them taken away, and they shortly returned, having been the victims of rape. They were completely petrified, screaming and in tears, shaking very badly. Their relatives and friends tried to console them. It was simply not human.

They had a game of passing some men through the opening of the wall, suggesting that they were being let free, just to be killed as they went to the assumed freedom. When one of those people, a hero, would try to protest, the end of a rifle would be pushed into his mouth and he would be shot – the end of another life.

All those beasts were completely drunk, gun-happy, roaming around us the whole night with torches and revolvers in their hands.

With the break of day, we were still in a state of helpless anger, confusion and fright. What could we expect next? The order came that we had to go to the nearest station, to be loaded on to cattle wagons and transferred to a 'transit' camp at Pruszkow.

On arrival, we found an enormous camp, completely wired round. It contained thousands of Poles, collected from the defeated part of Poland. There they were segregated according to whether they were political or ordinary civilians. However, we were assumed, as 99 per cent of us were families of Polish officers, to belong to that first category – political. As such, we were ushered separately and almost immediately, to be loaded on to another train (cattle-type, of course), to be taken 'somewhere'. It was the beginning of work camps for women and concentration camps for men.

Why we were considered like that, no one knows. Nobody asked us any questions at any time. Perhaps, if we had not been in such a terrible mental condition after the ordeal of the first night, then we could have made some stand and asked questions – perhaps we would have been freed.

However, in the end, perhaps, because we cared for our friends, who certainly needed protection, we boarded the train like cattle, watched by the armed SS, and the doors were sealed. The high-level wired windows, was the only contact with the world outside. Perhaps two, or three times, the train would stop somewhere surrounded by fields, and carriage by carriage, we would be let out to relieve ourselves – both sexes together, completely in the open.

It was a very long journey and no food was given, but fortunately, we had some with us. We travelled for two days and a night – I am not sure of the exact time. Eventually, we arrived at Oranienburg, near Berlin. It was a very large camp for both sexes. We were given some drink and bread, together with a portion of margarine. We were then put to sleep on a communal, very wide, wooden bed, probably for one hundred or more bodies, lying side by side. We did not know who slept next to us, except that we tried to keep our friendly groups together. This was another experience. However, we slept only up to early morning, at which point general segregation took place. Firstly, the segregation of males and females, and secondly, for those who appeared dangerous and those who did not. For that, we would all be totally stripped, and would go through a procedure that would become so familiar to me later.

Already realising that this would be the last time we would see our women friends, whom we had tried so hard to defend, I passed to my friends all the valuables I had, to keep. Somehow, I realised that we men would be deprived of all our possessions. I was right.

After being stripped, we went through the routine of being shaven of all our hair, even from around our private parts. This was performed by women wardens. It was the first direct humiliation. We later found that the women prisoners were similarly treated, but attended by male wardens.

Our women guards, with canes in their hands, which they used very liberally, asked us to dress again in our clothes, but before that, we were divided by sight into two groups.

My group, as I found later, was the concentration camp group, the others went to civilian working camps. This to myself, and I am sure to the reader, is beyond understanding.

The last night we spent almost entirely in an underground shelter, because of the American air raid on Berlin. We had a magnificent view of the scene, of thousands of searchlights, bombs being dropped and fires all over Berlin. It was at least some encouragement for us that the Germans were not spared the 'pleasure' of air attack. Some of the American planes were shot down, but for the first time we had some satisfaction, even without knowing what the next year would bring for us, and also not knowing what happened to the rest, especially the vulnerable womenfolk.

Next day our party was put on another train and taken not very far away to Sachsenhausen – the first of five concentration camps I 'attended'.

It was a very hot day; we had all our best and warmest clothing on us, and had to carry all our belongings in suitcases. In that condition we had to walk about two miles, from the station to the camp. Why we carried all that load – which in a few hours would all be taken away for ever – I do not know. However, that was the great unknown – there was always hope! It was very significant, and it was a situation when we saw no logic, nor any planned German future for us. Perhaps we should have tried even in that situation to make some attempt to preserve one's life by escaping? That was the situation which, nowadays, has been explained by psychoanalysts like Dr Bruno Bettelheim, as the effect of being stunned by the terror, applied to us by the SS. Our will to react was removed from our minds; we became kind of robots, even if for a limited period of time.

During our two mile walk, loaded with belongings, totally breathless, we could not think about anything other than getting there, when we would rest. Our destination was Sachsenhausen concentration camp. What an irony that we were actually dreaming of getting there.

We arrived at Sachsenhausen's gates. This I must describe, because it was a unique experience.

We were ushered in, in small groups, into a large barracks. There were several tables with SS officers sitting down and taking some notes. The procedure was astonishing. At the first table we would be asked to clear everything from our pockets and put all items on the table. It was unbelievable. Our money, fully accounted, pens, watches, rings, cameras, wallets, letters, etc. All would be fully listed. We would be shown that list and asked to sign it, to verify its accuracy. These would then be placed in special, mothproof bags, with our new number and name written on it, and we would then be asked to go to the next table. There, all our clothes would be carefully listed, collected and placed on hangers, again in large mothproof bags, and sealed again, with our name and number on it, and once more we would be asked to sign the list. At the last table, we arrived almost nude –

we had been asked to retain our leather belts. This was a very valuable item throughout our existence in all camps, as it was the only means to support our trousers.

At this last table, we would have to make our personal statement: name, date of birth, place of birth and all political facts. It was extremely difficult to remember everything. Similar statements had to be made in three of the five camps I was in.

The principle of German organisation was that all concentration camps were divided into main camps and so-called commandoes, which were the branches of the main camp. Whenever you were transferred to another main camp, all your belongings and papers would also be transferred. Your statement would be very carefully checked and compared with the previous one, and God help you if you slipped on that.

After the interrogation there was another shaving, bath and new uniform, which we will know for the next twelve months or so. Next, to the barracks and into the hands of people, or I would not use that term 'people' – rather creatures from one's worst nightmares. We were then given a big initiation sermon, bed allocation and rest.

We had to acquaint ourselves with our new conditions. They need some explanation, to make the reader realise how the best of our camps were organised.

The large barracks housed probably 300 to 500 people. There were two blocks of bunk beds, about four storeys high, with, say, six bunks' width and about ten in length. That meant about 480 people. But as many beds housed two bodies the total number could be much greater.

As I have already said, it was our best camp. In fact it was a show camp for the official visits from the Red

Cross. I do not know what their opinion was about conditions in the camp. Certainly, they would notice:

a) beautifully kept green lawns and flower beds.

b) very well-provided sporting areas for football, volley ball, tennis, etc.

c) symphony and brass band orchestras.

d) a library provided, with all permitted books.

e) every morning, in each block, on the central table there would be placed daily papers – German, of course.

f) by walking around, you would see people lying about, reading books or papers, playing chess, or listening to music.

g) they – or some of them – would be impeccably dressed, their prison uniforms, well-tailored, some 'chosen ones' wearing good leather shoes, almost heaven on earth. Good luck to them.

Unfortunately, being a transit camp, we were there no longer than two or three days and then we were back into the cattle wagons.

However, the difference now was that in each of the wagons, both sliding doors would be open. Twenty-five or more would sit cross-legged facing each of the rear walls. In the middle, the width of the sliding doors, four SS soldiers on seats with sub-machine guns and a full sized machine gun fixed in the middle too. No chance of escape – and where to? The train would stop once when we could relieve ourselves. We were also given a drink and a portion of bread and margarine.

During the journey, if anybody would get cramp, he could lift up his arm, and not more than two on each side could stand up for five minutes.

I don't remember how long it took, but we arrived at our destination camp, of extremely inferior character, in Brucks, in Sudetenland. We disembarked and got into the camp. It was the first sub-commando camp.

We would then quickly go to the Appeal Platz, where every smaller group, led by the capos, would be scrupulously counted; and if luck was on our side, we would be immediately allocated our first work. On the other hand, we might have to wait hours, until the overall count would tally. In this camp the work was very uneven. Cleaning the outside of the latrines, cleaning the streets and washing the wooden floor twice daily so that it would be pure white. I wonder whether you have ever tried to make a white wood floor be white again, after 400 people in wooden clogs, or even barefoot, have crossed it only once! It is possible, but I suggest you do not take up the challenge.

Brucks was an almost indescribable place. It was built in a huge valley, which was constantly in fog, where the famous Herman Goering Werke operated. The work could not start before the fog lifted (about 10 a.m.) and stopped as early as 4 p.m. for the same reason.

I was working on building roads, operating a very large mechanical hammer; it was extremely hard work. The civilian Germans tried to help us a little with food, but it was very difficult because of the eagle eyes of the SS guards. The days became very cold, and once we thought we could wrap our blankets on directly to our skin, and keep a bit warmer – not so, it was quickly discovered, to our great and painful experience. Canes, of course, as I said earlier, were liberally used.

Already then, for the second time, I realised that should I have a chance of surviving these very severe conditions, I would have to make a definite and positive decision to do whatever was in my power to keep myself physically fit. This meant doing whatever extra work was available, and because of that, get as much food as possible. Doing extra work entitled one to double the ration, usually. Having made the decision, my mind became much freer and optimistic about the difficult future I was to endure. After all, I was trying to say to myself, 'You don't have to be a capo, or a murderer, to be one of those to survive these sometimes impossible conditions.' I stuck to it – often it was very difficult, but strong will helped to make it possible.

The other thing which helped to maintain personal esteem, the value of actually feeling like a human being, was personal hygiene. From the beginning, we decided in our group, that every day we would shave ourselves. With great difficulty, we managed to get a razor blade. There were two barbers in our block, who would shave us (a group of about forty), using the same blade fixed in a split piece of wood. Every day we would sharpen the blade on a piece of stone. It was very uncomfortable, and painful at times. It may have been painful, but at the same time one got the feeling of being human beings, which means being of some personal standing, when we faced our life in the concentration camp. This helped us tremendously and was a contributory factor to our survival.

We always remembered those stylish clothes in Sachsenhausen, being not only cleaned, but pressed daily. This also helped us to aim not to let ourselves down.

It is now time to spell out that these personal conditions differ even nation to nation. Later on, I remember, we were in camps where people would have to be kicked out of their bunks by the capos. They were not ill, but simply tired. They lost their will to live. For as long as we could survive, we could look after ourselves. This in fact became the motto of many of us. We observed Germans, Russians or Poles washing themselves early in the morning, during the cold winter, in the freezing water. By seeing that, we understand what we meant by what we were saying, and we tried not to lose our dignity.

We knew very well what was meant by maintaining our dignity. We already knew that personal hygiene was the basic factor in this process.

Every day, I remember, we passed by a huge POW camp of Russian prisoners. They had been working very hard, appeared very healthy and seemed well prepared to face their difficult life. They were clean, tidy and shaven, and with very good morale – they were always singing Russian folk songs. This gave me a very good lesson for the remaining months, in all the concentration camps.

Today, it is well known that Hitler's idea was to destroy everyone's personality, by terror. I would say that in the majority of cases he had succeeded. Hitler even managed to subordinate, in a similar way, some of the dissidents in his SS forces. So always looking after personal hygiene would be sufficient for our survival, but was also to combat the continual terror which we had to learn to resist.

We were to be fully responsible for looking after our provisions. Next, the sanitation, which was at the end of the block. The use of it was most difficult at night, as the gaps between the floors in the bunks were minute. I managed to find myself in desperation only once. I found my place, but I would not risk it again, especially against the grumbling of the other prisoners.

We went to the kitchen block where our ration of one day's food would be given. This consisted of a small wedge of bread, a little portion of margarine and soup. This last item varied day by day in consistency, but was always made of some concoction of turnips, nettles and some other vegetable or even weeds. It could be like water or completely solid, so that you had to use your fingers to eat it. Some of my fellow prisoners ate the ration in one go – this was a bad habit, some tried to hide it in their pocket, wrapped in a piece of newspaper, and some simply did not know what to do with it. They did not even understand any German. We had one Ethiopian, who looked like Haile Selassie, and who was completely lost.

On a Sunday, there was no work, but we were told of a very strict bath time, in the evening. 'You must be hygienically clean, that is the first principle, of maintaining your health.' The next day, however, we found what seemed like millions of lice in our clothes, and most of our free time was sacrificed for the systematic killing of lice, before they would infect us with typhoid, or simply destroy us.

The following morning at 4 a.m., everyone was up, and the acclimatisation had begun. Firstly, there was the queue for the toilet, which was one large room, with probably ten seats and urinals along the perimeter. I could not tell you what we had to walk over, to reach one of the horrible loo seats, and there was no paper either. The stench was beyond belief. Next was the washroom; it was outside, thank goodness. You would have to keep a very careful watch on your clothes and equipment, otherwise you would be left nude and without food. Mind you, the bare bottom was more suitable for the heavy cane, which was used constantly. Breakfast was made up of the remains of your bread and margarine from the day before, and a cup of warm nettle-type tea.

As I said earlier, Brucks was an exceptional place for many reasons, but especially because it was extremely difficult to contain and control all prisoners, because of the almost constant fog. We very often heard planes overhead, of either the American or British air force, flying towards Berlin or some other German city. There would be alarms, anti-aircraft guns. There would also be some escapes over the nearby Czech border.

This was the first camp, in fact, where for the first time I witnessed a hanging. It involved four prisoners, who had tried to escape across the Czech border. They were hanged in full view of the whole camp. Apparently, it was usual practice; the frame was too short, so that after the kick-board was removed the victim just stood on the ground. Their legs would then be lifted and tied to the post; that is how they died. I was to see this performance on many occasions subsequently.

Fortunately, after one and a half weeks, we were moved to another main camp in Flossenburg, in Sudetenland. The camp had been built on the slopes of the stone quarry, on each level of which barracks were built, linked by steps at least twelve inches high, so that the prisoners would have sufficient exercise. On the arrival, as at every new camp, our clothes would be exchanged for new ones, after which we would 'enjoy' the ritual of the bath. The old clothes would be steam cleaned to kill the lice.

This time, it was a special experience. A shower-type

bath for about 300 people had just been constructed underground. We had to stand in the nude, under personal sprinklers, while the SS and capos would be checking for the straightness and lining of all prisoners, so that each of us would be directly under the sprinkler. The sprinklers themselves would be slightly dripping with cold water, for some people this was quite beyond their mental endurance – something the SS men were waiting for. They brought two of their victims to the raised platform, and after giving us a long sermon, they slowly murdered those two men before our eyes. This was a terrifying experience.

We did not know whether the dripping water would suddenly change to boiling hot or turn freezing cold. Each of us was given a tiny piece of soap (it was sand mixed with grease). The water was actually bearable, and we washed ourselves as well as possible. The SS, and capos, had already had their prize, therefore they were much more lenient. Obviously, every one of them would receive a new 'star'.

No drying out was possible of course. We were ushered to the next room, where new clothes were distributed.

Looking back on it now, this was real pandemonium – as the clothing was distributed to us, not by size, but by availability. It was up to us to use our initiative and to exchange the sizes between ourselves. However, there were some left who would not fit into any of the leftover uniforms. Then, even the horrible capos would try to help them, by bringing some new sizes. The shoes provided, were an even greater problem. I do not know exactly how such shoes were constructed, but the wooden sole had a kind of canvas top nailed to it.

I do not remember what I was doing in this camp, but I know that I was not there more than one to two weeks, and most of that time was sacrificed for the new registration procedure. The most difficult of the work I remember was to carry the water cans over the high steps described. Also, I remember that this was the only place where we received, only once, thick cabbage soup – but no spoon. Can you imagine, anyone, very hungry and in this situation? There was, to lighten our feelings, brass band music being played by a prison orchestra.

There were two things that struck me as being important. Firstly, that in this camp existed a prisoner with the number 0001. He was the first person I saw who had survived the whole duration of the camp. He was, of course, a German criminal of the lowest kind. When I said he was wearing number 0001, I should have explained that in the majority of camps, the number of prisoners would never exceed the theoretical capacity of the camp. It was, therefore, decided by the SS that when the first four figure number was reached, they would restart at the beginning.

Some camps would maintain records of the earlier numbers and they would not start afresh when the numbers reached 9999. Obviously, by this method they confused the judgement by the International Red Cross, which was searching for the whereabouts of various prisoners.

The other very significant happening was during the short stay in Flossenburg, where I must have been doing some quarrying work. I was on the verge of collapse, when a helping hand came from a Caucasian Russian. He was a farmer from the Swastopol area. His family had a smallholding that was barely big enough to survive on after paying the prescribed quota to the government. They, of course, cheated the authorities. The pigs' ear rings would be transferred to the young ones, and the old ones would be slaughtered, unbeknown to the authorities. I am very thankful to that Russian.

Beyond the barbed, electrified wire, we could see another barracks for women prisoners, for which pleasures one could earn a ticket, if you were a 'good' capo.

Incidentally, in this camp, there were a group of junior capos, who were trained in gaining points by various methods of murdering prisoners. Some methods were very refined. For instance, they would go to the toilet area and, for any reason, they would insert the end of a high pressure water hose into the rectum of a victim; until blood and the rest would appear at their mouth. I would never believe that a human being could do such a thing, if I had not seen it with my own eyes.

It was amazing, but all human beings of the bad category can be judged by the fact that some of them would kill a person in cold blood. The others would always, if they did not have a reason, try to find one; they would convince themselves that it is inevitable that for the safety of others, the person must be got rid of.

For instance, the Russians would not kill anyone (unless on the battlefield) if he or she would not confess to the almost imaginary or often invented crime. But they would go to great lengths of difficulties to prove such a case.

The Germans could be divided into two categories of those who were cold-blooded murderers. Their excuse was that they were doing it for their country, and because they were frightened. However, the majority again would have to have, if not proof, then at least an incentive, to make their blood boil. One such example was in the first camp: the block capo, one of the worst criminals, spotted one of the prisoners stealing from the heap of cut bread one small portion, which was not yet allocated to anyone. The capo got him out of the crowd, out of many people queuing for their rations. The capo delivered to the prisoners a very long lecture on morality. He was arguing that the prisoner could be responsible for the lives of 'poor little souls' who could not defend themselves. His excitement was visibly making his blood boil, eventually to such an extent that he murdered the prisoner. This he assumed to be his 'great moral principle of justice' (he was the capo, a convicted murderer several times over, admitted by himself), and he actually became a hero in his own eyes.

It is strange to me that this principle of life was held by so many otherwise, by all appearances, good people. I have witnessed many such cases, where the life of the individual became a cover to the murderous instincts of people – to see the blood appearing, and the life disappearing from completely innocent people. However, such individuals would always have on their conscience similar crimes already committed in the past.

Shortly, we were moved again, this time our destination was a sub-commando camp in Hersbruck, near Nuremberg. I consider this place the worst of all.

The reason why I felt that this was the worst camp was:

a) it was mostly occupied by Poles, who were ordinary prisoners, but at the same time, many of them performed capos duties.

b)   the camp was built on marshland, the blocks were built on piles and the German soldiers and officers would use the timber plank walkways, as would some of the privileged block 'elders'. We, on the other hand, would have to walk on the marshy land, often losing our shoes. There were approximately 3,000 men, but about 50 per cent stayed in the *revier* (hospital).

The death rate was probably one hundred per week, or even more. But the total number of prisoners was always the same.

The work consisted of cutting forests, placing soak-away drains, working in shallow iron mines, a concreting plant, and also, for some who were chosen as specialists, to work in the repair shop in a small-gauge railway to the mine. Except for not working in the mine, I experienced all other trades.

The first was in the repair plant. I of course, declared the ability to work on the foot-operated lathe, which I had used in my grammar school time. Apart from that, I had never in my life seen a twenty-foot electric modern machine. I was given a couple of hours of introduction and training by a civilian French worker, who did his best to use my abilities, but afterwards I was left to my own devices. I managed to exist in this workshop for two weeks (this entitled me to the extra ration). I repaired bolts, bearings, drilling holes, etc. The test came when the German engine driver came to me, asking me to help him to repair a broken whistle. 'No problem,' I said. I fixed it wrongly into the machine and it landed through the roof in the garden next door; it was only because it was the German's fault in the first place that I got away with it.

The second was more serious. I was asked to make a composition for the new bearings for the axle to an engine. With my 'intelligence', I managed to point out how the composition should be cut out. Unfortunately, I used the wrong cutters! The German foreman somehow liked me, which was fortunate. However, the next day, I was sent to lay drains in the sloping side of the forest. The German method was to lay the drains in the trough, on very prickly branches of wild rose bushes, before being filled up with light soil. With bare hands and the very cold weather, this was not suitable for me, and even the capos had to agree, after seeing my hands.

After that, I was already very weak, and I was directed to the concreting plant. They simply asked me, 'Do you know anything about reinforced concrete?'

The reply was obviously, 'Yes, of course.' What I was not aware of, was that the work consisted of carrying water to the concrete mixer in large wooden barrels. Carrying it with a colleague, we had to walk briskly about 200 yards there, and 200 yards back. After several rounds, my strength had vanished and I collapsed. I was carried to the camp hospital, where there were already 1,500 men. All occupied small beds, four patients in each, two one way, and two the other way.

At the reception, I was examined by a Ukrainian prisoner/*felcher* (nurse). He looked at my hand, and spotted the blue vein running up my arm. I do not know why, but he decided to inject me with the last of his antibiotic (penicillin had not been discovered yet). This man saved my life! To this day I have a mark on the top of my wrist, where the ulcerous infection started.

Immediately afterwards, I was seen by an old Polish doctor/prisoner, who looked at me, examined me and found that I was suffering from pneumonia, with fluid in my left lung. He was an extremely good man. He extracted one full glass of fluid from me, and gave me some pills. I was directed to bed by a young capo, who was, I am sorry to say, a very young Polish boy, the blue-eyed boy of the hospital. Unfortunately, he was, even in his early years, very cruel to the other prisoners, or perhaps, I would prefer to say, I have already forgotten the facts.

Every concentration camp was equipped with several crematoria. These were usually placed out of sight of the inmates, but you could not help smelling the fumes of cremated bodies. We did not talk much in the camp, but the crematorium always provided some comments: perhaps, because like any other working party, there were groups of our 'mates' assisting there too. Some of those burning places were extremely primitive, but some were highly refined, where the different valuable parts of the human body would be utilised. Sometimes, for the production of soap, fertilisers and of course for the experiments. It is not a nice subject to write about, and we certainly did not indulge in talk of it, but from time to time someone would come with the news of the latest information.

Our minds were already very blank, to cope with such emotional information. I often think, when watching films on television of POW camps, how different the way of life was there. How much their life was buzzing with excitement, with every minute piece of news. It is obvious to me why there are no such films about how life really was in concentration camps. They would be disgustingly boring and would, ironically, appear unreal.

People don't realise what life in concentration camp

looked like. I will try to give you an example of one day in Hersbruck.

One would be woken up at daybreak. The junior capos would be running along the rows of bunks, shouting and hitting with a cane to wake the prisoners. With hardly any noise, like automatons, the prisoners would drop to the floor from their bunks. There would be a procession and queue to the toilet and cold washing taps. The brave ones would strip and try to revive themselves with a shower of cold water. Meanwhile, a lot of people would still be in their bunks, unable to collect enough energy to lift themselves and step to the ground. Ninety per cent would have gone to sleep exactly in the condition as they came from work the previous day.

The capos' canes, proved almost always successful to bring those people to reality. There would usually be a problem of missing boots, or caps, or jackets, or even laces to the boots. Warm liquid would be served and everybody ushered to the Appeal Platz. There, all the 3,000 prisoners would be arranged in blocks by their capos, then the count would begin. It could take from half an hour to two or even three hours, until all the prisoners have been accounted for. This, of course, included the dead prisoners, who had to be brought to the count too. Then the sorting out would begin. You would have to remember your number well. Different commandoes would be arranged, and under escort of SS and *Wehrmacht* soldiers, we would walk to work.

Late in the afternoon, the gradual return of working parties to the same Appeal Platz would begin. Some of the parties would be carrying improvised stretchers with the dead. Again, counting – many, many times.

After that, if there was to be an execution, we would

all have to wait to witness the hanging.

Later, return to the barracks for the much-needed and deserved soup, bread and margarine ration.

If anybody had enough strength to wash, they did so, and then to bed. It was a typical day. Of course, it depended on individual health conditions how one could make the best of that day. Certainly capos and block leaders were well groomed and fed; their life was not only bearable, but quite well organised indeed.

There were two incidents in Hersbruck when I was in the hospital, which certainly added more to my already well-built experience; and in addition, built further my resilience to hear, see and to endure the difficulties in my life.

There were cases of people being very ill indeed, with inflammation of the legs, with open ulcers, which were an everyday issue, and in many instances, the first step to the ultimate death.

One day, a man was brought to our compartment. It was one of the capos with gangrene affecting his legs. The only solution was amputation. There were no anaesthetics and almost no bandages or surgical tools. However, they briefed and arranged the hospital staff, organised a improvised operating table, and in our view, by holding the man with a scarf across his mouth, his leg was amputated, the blood vessels tied, the bone cut with some kind of hacksaw. The leg was disinfected over the fire, and the skin was sewn across the stump of the leg. The procedure was repeated with the other leg. Water was poured across the poor man's face. He survived the operation, but was dead by the following morning.

The following day, or the day after, I witnessed on the same table another operation. This time, it was to chisel out a hole behind the patient's ear, in order to remove a tumour – don't ask me how they managed to diagnose the existence of a tumour.

Again, with colossal screams, the operation was an apparent success, but the patient died the following day.

Shivers go through my spine, even today, when I am writing these stories. It was unbelievable.

It was only possible to carry out such operations because those people were so important to the life in the camp. All 'medical' staff would carry out every kind of operations or treatment – in order to save their own skins. The doctors I saw would never have performed such operations, without knowing that their lives were at stake too.

In my bed, where there were four ill prisoners, two in each direction, movement was extremely difficult; however, we managed. The unfortunate thing I experienced was that I woke up twice with a cold body next to me – it was that of a dead man. I could call it another of those experiences linked to my life in concentration camps.

Incidentally, before I landed in this hospital, in my block with the capo, another Pole, there were peculiar incidences.

This capo, like a few others, tried to prove to the others how caring they were, how much they tried to make the SS men cooperate and make our life 'easier'. Once, I remember, the SS officer came in the evening. He was treated to a drink or two. The capo asked us to feel very patriotic and to start singing traditional Polish songs. The SS officer joined in the celebration. It was not only peculiar, it was also very cruel.

Firstly, we were extremely tired, trying to think about

tomorrow's work. Secondly, we were very hungry and the singing of patriotic songs would not make our lives any better. What is more, I saw him (the capo) delivering twenty or thirty hits from the cane to some prisoners, because in his opinion they had misbehaved. You should have seen them afterwards. There were many such incidents.

Back to the hospital. After a few days, the directive came that the whole hospital would be loaded on the train to go further south.

The order meant to load all sick prisoners on to open rail wagons. The wagons had sides less than two feet and six inches in height, not meant to carry people. But we were loaded, standing body to body, one hundred to a wagon. The train started and all the standing people tried to keep upright by supporting one another. We did not expect to have to endure that indignity for more than two full days and nights. We were without water and food and there were no toilet facilities.

Gradually people's legs started to give in and, one by one, the weakest would drop to their knees and to the floor. The stronger people kept standing for longer, but even they succumbed to the strain and were forced to sit – yes, to sit – on those heaped bodies, many of them already dead.

When the train stopped on the sidings in Dachau the situation was tragic. Out of 1,000 sick prisoners, only a handful from each of the wagons had survived. We, the survivors, had to scramble over hundreds of dead bodies to get to the platform. We were herded to the barracks, given a drink, had a very short rest, then were sent back to work.

I suddenly developed a great pain in my abdomen and,

by sheer luck, a capo took pity on me and carried me to the camp hospital. It was thanks to that help that I survived this particular episode of concentration camp life. I will never forget the pain and the indignity we suffered.

As a postscript to that episode, the camp hospital in Dachau was maintained as a showcase for the Red Cross inspection. It was my great luck to be there. To my amazement, I found myself on a spring bed, with a mattress, sheets, pillows and blankets. The prison doctors arrived. Two of them were expert surgeons, one Czech and one Hungarian. They examined me and decided that I should have my appendix removed. However, they told me in secret that there were rumours that the American army was already approaching very rapidly and it would not be very safe for me to be either during or just after an operation, to be bedridden, should the war be upon us.

So they decided to keep me in bed for the time being, with some medication. This 'unfortunately' improved my condition and there were no signs of any American army. On the contrary, I overheard that it might be possible for me to be released from the hospital. This simply terrified me. It was all right for them, but unfortunately, I knew the condition of the main camp.

Ironically it was a great relief to me when, suddenly, a large batch of seriously wounded prisoners arrived. I recognised among them a number of my friends from Hersbruck, who were allocated to a walking party, because of their relatively healthy condition, to walk to Dachau. According to their story, they had been machine-gunned by the American planes, who had mistaken them for a German military convoy.

I offered my services immediately, to attend to the

wounded, saying that I had male nurse experience in this field (scout training). I attended very serious cases, and at the same time I learnt how to be useful in such desperate situations.

Soon afterwards, a typhoid epidemic started to spread in Dachau. The Germans opened a new block which was to be completely isolated – with double barbed wire – from the rest of the camp.

They were looking for three volunteers to run this block. I was, of course, the first; there was a Jewish doctor, and to my great, surprise, Mr Bitny-Schlachto, a colleague and friend from my grammar school days in Kielce.

In this new block, we had about 350 ill patients, with both types of typhoid. We were supplied with at least thirty-five new cases daily – alas, approximately thirty-five were dying daily. We really worked very hard. The Germans would give us as much medicine as they could, the best food they could afford. All this was provided into a neutral zone, between the two lines of barbed wire. The only people allowed into this no-man's-land area, were body carriers, and food and medicine providers. Those things would be left in between the two fences, until all gates would be closed.

The three of us found ourselves entirely isolated from the main camp. With the help of the Jewish doctor, we divided the work and the shifts so that we could devote as much as possible time to the ill, and at the same time, not lose our strength completely.

I had never been immunised against any type of typhoid, nor the other two, but I would not tell this to anybody, oh no!

I was allocated the job of medical care, including temperature charts, some night duties, and the most important one, giving medicines and injections. After daily inspections, the doctor gave me a list of cases; the beds were all numbered, for when the injection was to be given. We had a large steriliser electrically connected, several syringes and a limited number of injection capsules. We also had very few antibiotics, the rest were rather to restore the physique of the ill. Some were under the skin, some intramuscular and some intravenous.

I had no difficulties giving the first two types of injections. However, never in my life had I given an intravenous one. I had received them perhaps five or six times myself, either for calcium or some other vitamins. Here, however, I was faced with several types, and also I was faced with people whose veins were almost stringy and very hard. Nevertheless, it was life or death to me. Therefore, I had to pluck up my courage and attend to my first patient. I knew the procedure; the most difficult part was to find the vein, pierce it, draw a small amount of blood and then carry out the injection.

It took me almost the whole thirty minutes to do the first one. I was sweating all over myself. The next patient waiting was almost running for the doctor. This probably helped me to make a decisive move. It was done! The doctor arrived and said, 'Well done, in the circumstances, a very difficult vein.'

Eventually, I was giving forty injections daily, and of those, five to ten were intravenous. From that first day, there was no trouble at all.

Although we worked extremely hard, with better food my strength was slowly regaining some stability. I was still very ill, with my legs swelling badly, mostly due to Hersbruck's marshy conditions, but, otherwise I felt that

I was on the mend. This, of course, depended on many conditions, which were completely outside my control.

Firstly, I could catch the typhoid. Secondly, the Germans could decide, as was very much on everyone's lips, to burn the whole block and get rid of the typhoid. Also, I could make a mistake, and that would ruin my reputation and my existence on this ward. There could be many other reasons.

There was also the question of actually coping with some of the ill. We had many cases of people getting mad, with fits beyond control; we had to restrain them, in fact, by tying them to their beds. Many times it was almost impossible for the three of us to do the work. We used to co-opt some of the lucky ones who had survived the typhoid with our help to assist us. This helped us tremendously. We used them to help with the toilet duties and with keeping temperature charts, which were very important in the medication. They did this work very gratefully.

At the end, when Dachau was freed, by the Seventh American Army, there were still nearly 300 prisoners alive in our block.

The American army arrived, fully equipped with all the DDTs, etc. They could not believe that neither I nor my colleague had been immunised against any type of typhoid. We were injected by them, and it nearly killed us. We were later told that the first American soldier who entered Dachau was a Pole. I remember, too, how the Americans asked to slaughter all the pigs from the German HQ, to make soup, which unfortunately killed many who were simply too weak for such rich food.

There were funny moments too. As I said earlier, we were provided with the best food, which could be obtained by even depriving some German SS of it. It proved how terrified they were of typhoid spreading among themselves.

Most of the patients could hardly eat anything; they drank milk and could eat a small quantity of semolina. To return the milk or other valuable food to the Germans would be a complete waste; it would only be thrown away, as they feared contamination. Therefore, from time to time, we would have a proper feast. No one knew about it, because no one would dare to enter our block. This was ironically funny, in some sense. However, we felt that we had given all we could of ourselves; therefore, we deserved some reward from time to time and we had no regrets.

When the American army came in, the first who entered our block was an officer. He sat on a little table and, after a few preliminary questions, offered me a cigarette – Pall Mall. I could not refuse, I had not had one for nearly a year, but certainly never as strong as Pall Mall cigarettes were. I nearly collapsed after a few puffs. He realised, and took the cigarette from me. 'I'm sorry,' he said, 'it was very stupid of me.'

'But nevertheless, I have enjoyed it,' was my reply.

He spoke good German, and as neither I, nor my colleagues understood any English, that was the language we used. We learnt the general military position from him and how he thought our future would be. He also told us that they did not know about Dachau, but someone had told them of such a camp, somewhere in the area, and that was how they had found us.

I also remember how the American reporters, men and women, flew into Dachau, and took photographs of dead bodies, which had been arranged. I still have a print of one of those photographs. The Americans were completely bewildered when they inspected the rows of cremation ovens. We were very quickly whisked to Munich, to the HQ of the SS Training Centre. There were enormous buildings, fully decorated with 'Hitler's World History'. On all corridors there were paintings of Teutonic figures, dominating the rest. As the story goes, the führer said that he did not like it, and the architect, on hearing this verdict, committed suicide by jumping from one of the turrets.

In this enormous building, the Americans organised the systematic identification and records of all 40,000 or so inhabitants of Dachau. It was an almost impossible task.

First, the Vatican took care of the 500 priests, who had been kept in one block in Dachau. Then the Czechs and Jews did the same with their people. They were all extremely well organised. We Poles were some of the last. I knew of the location of Jola and she knew of my existence by one or two letters from my mother, and from the communication from the Red Cross. Sitting in the transit camp in Munich, organised by the Seventh American Army, was very boring indeed. We were walking, still in our concentration camp uniforms, along the streets of Dachau, and the Germans very kindly, bewildered, removed anything that was in our way (this of course included field telephone cables of German or American origins).

I can assure you that such shyness in the German defeated would not last very long and we had been warned by American army officials to be very careful of any fraternisation, at this stage. It was very important that we were unarmed.

To conclude this chapter, I would like to add that one day, I went by train to Murnaw, where there was a Polish POW camp. It was on the southern border of Bavaria. I did not go to the camp, but I went very close to it to see the beautiful view of the Alps; it was breathtaking. I had to thank God for being alive.

The other incident was still in Dachau. The Jewish community invited an American cantor for a concert. We were invited by our doctor who, as you may remember, was a Jew. The concert was beautiful and very moving indeed.

In addition to my postscript to the life in the concentration camps, I have to add one observation:

After being freed by the Americans, but before being moved from Dachau, we used to wander along the camp area, often trying to find any friends. In fact, we found quite a few who came all the way from Warsaw in our group. They were needed, later, when the American authorities tried to issue us with some kind of passes. These passes would not only identify us, but would also give a brief history of our movements. For that we required witnesses who would, by their signatures, verify such statements.

However, the reason for writing this epitaph is different. When walking among the prisoners in Dachau, I was sure I saw many of the capos, who tortured us and other prisoners. We had neither strength nor energy to proceed with denouncing those people. I know now that it was wrong, but at the time being free meant more to us than anything. We could then even forget the atrocities that we had witnessed or experienced. It was not only my opinion, but that of the majority of ex-prisoners opinion.

I know that this chapter could be more than doubled

in its descriptive contents, but being gruesome it gave me the feeling that it contains details detested by most people as an inhumane way of treating your fellow human beings, independent of whether you like them or not. I have often wondered whether it is good to talk about the atrocities done by Germans (or the Japanese or English, or any other nation), whether they could ever be justified.

People often say that the new generations are looking with different eyes at what they have to face in the world. To those of yesterday they are much more understanding, they say. But are they? I think that young people today are already much more focused on today's way of life and therefore accept what was done yesterday as an inevitable fact of life.

This is in fact why I, and I am sure, many others, do not want to talk about our experiences.

My children, for instance, assumed that it was my bad luck that I landed in a concentration camp. They dream that a new life will be different, will bring love and happiness to us all – 'Let's forget about those horrible times.' In fact, they have no idea what times they were. Perhaps, these few pages will give them some outlook of what I, and many others, have gone through.

My son tells me that it was for some reason a taboo subject in our house, but why? He knows very well that neither he nor his sister wanted to know anything about it, about something that would upset them.

I said earlier that the records of the tragedies of life in the concentration camps are only in writing, or in one or two films. People do not want to be shown what was happening behind the electrified wires of Dachau or Belsen because it is so horrific that it might affect them or their children more than any X-certificate film.

However, it is the reality of such a life, which is not the result of an atom bomb but simply the consequences of a maniac leader like Hitler, or perhaps a Japanese general. That is where we suffered, and many more could suffer too, in the future. After all, history repeats itself. With Nero's cruelties in Rome, or any other acts of obscenity, even in the time of the inquisition.

We don't want to know of it, but unfortunately it happens, and it will happen again in the future.

An End to War and a Journey to England

I don't know whether I made myself clear before, but our being freed from Dachau was not at the same time as the end of the war.

The struggle between all armies against Germany and Italy was still in full progress, until the complete surrender on 30 April, when Hitler committed suicide in his bunker, in Berlin, and when the Victory in Europe Day was declared on 5 May.

I have to mention this date, because the attitude of the German civilians before the official surrender was completely different to that after this date.

The fear which the German citizens had at the earlier stage made them terrified. They did not know what to expect from the invading forces – American or British. On the other hand, after the Armistice, their morale was given a boost. They again became arrogant, almost dangerous. This fact is well described in Lady Ryder's book (Sue Ryder then), when she worked, trying to defend the lost DPs (displaced person) on the German soil.

When, after being liberated, we started to wander along the streets of Dachau, or later in Munich, we noticed how the attitude of the population had already very gradually deteriorated from a very positive, sympathetic or even fearful one to that which was and is known to us as that of the *herrenvolk* arrogance.

The shops and stores were completely empty. Not

Young days: from one year to fourteen

Young days

Young days

Family life in the 1920s and 1930s

Family life

Family life in 1920s and 1930s

Family life in the 1920s and 1930s

Family life in the 1920s and 1930s

Family life in 1920s and 1930s

Boy Scouts and Cadets

Our house bombed at the end of the war

Waiting for pass to cross the border from parts occupied by Russia to those occupied by Germany

College friends in Cracow

College friends in Cracow

1945 to 1947 in BAOR in Germany

1945 to 1947 in BAOR in Germany

*Jola, Mr Cumft and the author stepping down from the
National Gallery in London*

1945 to 1947 in BAOR in Germany

Starting out in London

Life in London – my new family

Visit to Poland with Maxine

My grammar school in Kielce revisited in 1984

Meeting old friends in Warsaw

Our cottage in Ixworth

having any money, we wouldn't have been able to buy anything anyway.

At the time we were very pleased with and proud of ourselves, survivors of such a tragic five years. That was why for some time, we would wear the concentration camp uniforms.

When we were transferred to the SS Higher Education Military College in Munich, we were, if I remember rightly, given some civilian clothes, and as I said earlier, full identification documents. There were, as we were informed, several possibilities for our future, as outlined by the American authorities. They generously offered any one of us a place in the USA, should we wish to live there rather than go back to Poland. Poland, as we already knew, was under full Russian rule, even having a Polish puppet regime.

We had endless discussions, wandering through the corridors of this curious building. There was the whole history of Germany as Hitler would have liked it to be; all in very dominant-type mural paintings. The whole history was, of course, completely distorted, but we were used to this. This is how history is taught today in Polish schools. All we know is that somewhere our true history will survive in its true interpretation and documentation. Or will that be true? Even today there are arguments over some historical fact that happened during our lifetimes.

I made myself, with great pride, a pair of shorts out of a canvas material. They eventually went with me to London.

However difficult it was to communicate during the war and after, we somehow managed to know of each other's whereabouts. During my stay in the concentration camps, I received two food parcels from my parents, and two letters, both from my mother. From those letters, and from my replies, the whereabouts of Jola was established, and conveyed to both of us.

Because of this information, I decided that instead of being enrolled to go to the USA, I would try to hitchhike to BAOR (the British Army of the Rhine), where I could find her.

I was fully prepared, and notified everyone of my intentions, when a message was conveyed to me, with great excitement: 'A jeep with two soldiers and two ATS women has arrived, and they are asking for you.'

It was of course Jola, along with her friend Maryla and her new husband Tadzik, and a corporal driver. It was a great moment. They were well received by the Polish commandant of the Polish section of the camp. Actually, the whole camp was buzzing with excitement, seeing British uniforms and a British jeep.

I was confronted with Jola, and, as it was always in her style, we were left alone to 'sort ourselves'. This took us four hours in the nearby countryside. She told me her story, and I told her mine. I learnt how she had managed to persuade the colonel of the regiment to let her, Maryla and her husband and a driver cover 1,000 kilometres in a completely unknown and still dangerous area of Germany – to find me.

I told her that, should they not have come that day, I would soon have been on my way to try to find her. Perhaps, in a rather more basic way, by hitchhiking, asking for help from German authorities, or asking the US army for help. There were endless possibilities, but I knew that I would have found Jola.

After long discussions, taking every possibility into

account, we decided that I would return with them to Maczkow (Harren). It was a great turning point in both my life and Jola's.

When we came back to the camp, or as it was, the large SS building, it was time for a short talk with the POW captain. He was a mine of funny stories, which one would accept with the proverbial tongue-in-cheek. But we all had a good laugh.

I know that it is in our Polish blood, that we like to boast about our past experiences, but it is equally my opinion, that there should be a limit to that. I think, looking back, he exceeded that limit – but good luck to him.

On the same day, we decided to start our journey back. After all, they had been on a limited leave from their unit, with great risk, and should anything go wrong, they might put the whole unit of BAOR force in a very precarious situation.

The journey of 1,000 kilometres in this almost completely devastated country was very difficult indeed. We stopped twice – once for the night, and once to have a rest. My friend, Tadzik, the second lieutenant of the Polish army under British command, did not know any German; therefore, it was left to me to command the Germans to give us adequate quarters for the night. He was trained to conquer; I was just released from being conquered. It was therefore very difficult for him to understand why I did not demand in a very strong voice and use equally strong vocabulary to make the Germans get what we required. Tadzik's revolver, uniform and jeep were in themselves sufficient to support our demands, which were always fulfilled without question. Later on, however, he always used to remind me of my weakness in being able to give orders. Perhaps by now, he fully understands my way of life.

This apparent shyness or lack of ability to control the situation when it is required or to give orders have, only recently, been explained to me by a television programme. It was a very interesting programme, about the life of a leading psychoanalyst, Bruno Bettelheim. He is an Austrian of Jewish descent, who was arrested by the German SS soon after Austria had been annexed by Hitler. He spent a very difficult year in the Dachau and Buchenwald concentration camps. After being freed he went to live in the USA, and for the last forty years has been working with children with emotional problems.

It is Bruno Bettelheim's opinion that the Germans were masters in terrorising prisoners, in the most refined ways. Such oppression is generally long-lasting, and is represented by nightmares, general indecision and a tendency towards withdrawal. He was given countless examples of such phenomena. It requires many years of studying oneself and a lot of self-control to make bad dreams gradually recede.

In my case I overcame some part of the after-effects of Gestapo oppression during my stay in the concentration camps, but every so often the nightmares in dreams return – perhaps I will have to put up with them.

Tadzik was very young, perhaps one or two years younger than I was, when he left Poland in 1939. As far as I know he landed in France and after their capitulation via Dunkirk, he found himself in Scotland. There he got his matriculation and cadet course, which after going into action in Normandy, gave him the rank of second lieutenant. He was well liked by the members of the officers' staff, as well as by the other ranks of his artillery unit.

He directed the fire of artillery during the invasion in a very successful way. He eventually married Maryla when the Polish army liberated the women's POW camp in Oberlangen.

His mother, who came from the work camp in Germany, was united with his father, who was a Polish officer, held in a POW camp. Unfortunately, he was very ill and soon died, without my knowing him at all.

His mother, however, arrived with them in England, and they lived together while Tadzik went through the resettlement corps and became a radio and television expert, with Marconi's training.

They are still living in London at the same address. Maryla and Tadzik both work at Harrods, where they have made a good name for themselves in their different departments.

We have been very good friends all this time and I sincerely hope we will stay like that for as long as we will live.

Anyway, back to my story. We arrived in Maczkow and I was left there for a short time before the verification would be completed and I would be officially enrolled in the Polish army under British command. This eventually happened and I was enrolled as a private. I had still to be verified as a cadet officer, with the rank of corporal. It took a little time, but eventually, even that bridge was crossed and I was accepted in the officers' mess as one of them.

Jola was a warrant officer, but when we got married, as my wife she was also treated as a member of the elite of the officers' ranks.

At the beginning I was stationed with Jola and another five girls in Maczkow, in the old bank building. They were quite comfortable quarters, perhaps one of the better equipped in the whole town of Maczkow.

It would be better to clarify the scene of this Polish town – Maczkow, which was originally known as Harren. As the Polish First Armoured Division, under General Maczek, liberated that part of Germany, and several POW camps and civilians in work camps, they decided to evacuate the small town of Harren of all its German inhabitants, and handed it over to the Polish ex-prisoners.

Out of the different camps, the Polish Woman's camp at Oberlangen consisted mostly of fighters from the Warsaw Uprising. They were taken prisoner after the collapse of Warsaw and went through several POW camps.

Most of the girls were from the Underground Army, and very many, like Maryla and Jola, were Girl Guides, working in sanitary units or hospitals, attending the wounded during the uprising.

I have already written quite a lot about scouts and guides, and probably I will be returning to this subject many times yet. A little digression will therefore not be out of place.

Recently, I watched a documentary film about Baden-Powell, which to me was very enlightening even with my wide experience. For instance, worldwide, there are just over 234 million scouts, yet when Hitler started his *Hitler Youngen* (a nationalistic movement, but similar to scouting), in about four years there were over 4 million of them – a very sorry story.

I am referring to that because in my grammar school, as in most similar ones, we had about 120 to 140 scouts, out of 900 boys. We had eleven patrols, and in summer the camp was attended by fifty to seventy boys. The school provided a special room for us with a permanent exhibition of various things connected with the movement.

During the 1939 to 1945 war, scouting in Poland was banned by the Germans and Russians, but it flourished secretly, just the same. This included training, camps and preparation for the future. This was a colossal contribution to the future Warsaw Uprising, which has been very well documented.

There were, of course, many boys and girls who would laugh at our ways, or at our wearing short trousers, but we always were supported by the majority and by the authorities.

Now, back to my story again.

Jola and I decided to get married, and this took place on 19 August 1945. There were no special celebrations. Actually, we had forgotten about the need for a ring, and this was done the day before by the silversmith next door, out of our silver spoons. He cheated us, because shortly afterwards brass appeared through the worn silver plating. I still have the rings; they are the only mementos of our happy marriage. Jola, as I will later describe, died on 4 August 1981 in London.

Maczkow, the promised living married quarters, by the quartermaster of the town, never materialised (he used to call them the 'Doves' Nest'). However, when I was recalled to my new unit in Bawinkel, we were allocated married quarters with a German farmer's family. They were very good and friendly people. They never changed their habits, war or no war. As all farmers were, anywhere, they were very well-off, or should I say, normal.

We were allocated a front room, and often we would sit with them in their main room, where the whole family would gather next to the fire.

The father sat on the nearest seat to the open fire, with his very long pipe resting on his toe.

We used to have supper with them. They would boil the typical German *wurst* (sausage), of which a large number would hang from the ceiling in the larder. They would be boiled with cabbage and other vegetables, and served very hot. It was rather unusual, but a very good meal.

Once, I remember, when looking at the farmer, I spotted quite a large carbuncle on his neck. It must have been rather painful for him. Having had my recent experience of the 'Dachau Hospital', I suggested that I could relieve him of this problem. I suppose the carbuncle was about two inches in diameter.

To my astonishment, he agreed. First of all, as I had never in my life performed such an operation (nor did I perform many others), I went to our First Aid Officer, to ask for advice and help. He told me that I was crazy, and the only thing he could do was to give me some local anaesthetics, lancet, tweezers, bandages and of course disinfectant. He warned me to be very careful. I arranged the day with the farmer, and I prepared all the essentials and asked everyone, excepting the farmer, to leave the room. After thorough cleaning, the anaesthetic, which was the spray type of ether, was applied. I performed the operation, cutting the carbuncle with a cross, opening it, and removing about ten roots. It must have been very painful to the farmer (he was over fifty years of age), but he stood up to it remarkably.

After cleaning and disinfecting the wound, I applied

the dressing and told him that he could relax. The ten roots I presented to him as a memento. The whole family, and I, of course, were totally amazed. I was congratulated. The patient recovered fully, in less than a week. We have been praised and admired friends ever since.

Jola and I decided that for once we had to have some celebration after our uneventful marriage. Therefore, after obtaining leave, we arranged to go to Brussels. There was one problem – to go to Belgium, you required Belgian currency. We had been paid by the BAOR in pounds, which were of no value in Belgium. Therefore, we had to exchange our money into some valuables, like diamonds or gold, to be able to exchange them for Belgian money in Brussels.

So we bought some diamond earrings that were rather substantial, and having been told that we would receive colossal exchange value, we set off on our honeymoon.

The diamonds, we were told, on our arrival in Brussels, were old-fashioned, and therefore we got very little money for them. But at least we had enough to have a happy week, visiting a completely reconstructed Brussels, with everything at its best, as if it were not just a few months after they had endured five years of war.

We went to cinemas, concerts and also on many sightseeing trips. We stayed in a reasonable hotel which was really good value.

The colossal difference in the style of life from occupied Poland, via concentration camps and then a rather poorly equipped BAOR, was an eye-opener. Today it is obvious – we know who is well-off and who has the economic power and completely reconstructed life. Germany, France, the Benelux countries, Switzerland

and even Italy. One can recognise such facts by going abroad and by staying in their hotels, enjoying meals and so on. It is a sad story.

In Brussels we saw the latest films from the USA, in first class cinemas. The concerts were well attended. It was like being in a completely different world. It was certainly not what was in store for us when we eventually landed in England!

When we saw the films, *Ziegfeld Follies*, *A Matter of Life and Death* or *Annie, Get Your Gun*, we felt that they represented life in Brussels at that time. Again, a very sad story.

I did not tell you that in Germany we acquired a little fox terrier – Leta. She was a very good friend. We left her alone when going to Brussels. On our return, she was sitting on our windowsill waiting. We found out later that she was so terribly lonely, that in desperation she chewed right through our bed. It was a rather tragicomic situation. We forgave her eventually.

Jola was still working in Maczkow, organising a boarding school for young displaced girls, to prepare them for their life, and also to give them a minimum of the required education.

On one occasion the River Elms, which embraced Maczkow, started to overflow its banks. This became one of the greatest floods I have ever witnessed.

In the beginning, I got leave from the unit at Bawinkel to go to Maczkow. I arrived on the banks of the over-flowing river, and realising that the Bailey Bridge, resting on pontoons which had replaced an earlier damaged concrete bridge, was starting to get submerged, I, and some other enterprising men, found some old biscuit tins, and by putting our shoes in them, and using them as wellingtons, we managed to cross over the already submerging bridge.

However, when we got to the other side, we were suddenly faced with a surge of water from the other side of Maczkow. It was simply terrifying to see. To go to the place where Jola was stationed with her pupils, I would have to swim across the street, to land on the other side, at first floor level. I managed that, and found that they had managed to transfer most of their provisions to the first floor, together with an improvised kitchen.

Thus we stayed, for over a week, until the water subsided. It reminded me of the time over ten years earlier, when I experienced a similar flood whilst on the scouting camp in Poland.

We eventually returned to the unit in Bawinkel. There the life was very idle and very boring indeed. I went shooting in the nearby forest. My duties included overseeing the other ranks of soldiers, who enjoyed themselves as much as they could by fraternising with the willing German girls, who would offer their graces and the rest for a packet of cigarettes, or even less. Our soldiers would suffer greatly with VD and only thanks to the recently discovered penicillin, would quickly be cured. Unfortunately, not for long!

I then learnt that there were prospects for me to continue my studies in structural engineering in London. So much so, that knowing that Jola was already in an advanced stage of expecting our first child, I risked going to London for two weeks. As it was to prove, it was a terrible waste of time. Firstly, I did not know any English, and that was the first condition of studying there. There were many other unknowns, like accommodation, how to care for Jola in Germany, and so on.

Therefore, rather disheartened, I decided to go back.

However, I must add one or two incidents. Firstly, on arrival at Victoria Station, I boarded bus number 174, I think to go to the army hostel for the night. I think it was run by the Salvation Army, somewhere along Victoria Street.

When I was sitting on the top deck of the bus, I noticed that the other passenger had a familiar face. It was my colleague from the grammar school in Kielce. Not only that, he had just arrived on two weeks' holiday from Rhodesia – what a coincidence.

With great difficulties, I visited several friends in London whose addresses had been given to me, and then I found my way to Victoria Station again. The army RTO directed me to the right train, and told me something I could not understand. What he in fact said was that somewhere I would have to change trains.

I fell asleep and was eventually awoken by the railway guard's lantern. He was inspecting the empty train, which was by this time, in a siding. I didn't even know the name of the station. It was certainly not near Dover, where I was to get my boat to Germany. This was a dead end line, and after finding an interpreter, I was directed to a local hotel to spend the night, because there were no further trains until the following morning. The next day, there would be a very complicated train service to take me to Dover.

I received a new ticket and a full list, giving the name of the station where I would have to change trains. Eventually, I arrived in Dover. There is no need to add, that besides arriving late to my unit, I eventually received a fat bill for my stay in the hotel and for the train ticket.

Worse was to come: I had arrived too late to witness

the birth of our first child, Ingrid. I was heartbroken. Fortunately, both mother and child were in good health, and my error was forgotten.

I had to work now, very quickly. Firstly, by finding a local craftsman who had a small steel workshop. I designed a child's cot, to be constructed out of very thin tubing, which could be totally dismantled, with a good mattress and stringy netting round it. It was finally painted in good white enamel, and it was so successful that it arrived, eventually, with us in England.

This particular craftsman also helped me to convert an ordinary pushchair into a pram. It was made from very thin metal sheets, also used for the canopy. The canopy would rotate, with the shape of the bottom of the pram. With the coat of nice paint and the well-made mattress, it was almost like a modern pram, with one drawback – it was very heavy, probably even bullet proof!

Also locally, I found a cabinet maker, who again, to my design, constructed two very large trunks, which had hinged shelves for shirts etc., and in the other half, provision for hanging dresses and suits. The bodies of the trunks were made of very thin plywood, as used in the glider industry. The works manager covered both trunks with a strong hessian cloth, and attached locks, handles, and leather straps, completing the job. These trunks were masterpieces, to everyone's envy. Even today, forty years hence, we have some remains of those trunks, serving as little cupboards or shelves.

I am saying all these things to emphasise how difficult it was then, in Germany, to get anything. None of the things described could be purchased in a shop at any price.

It was now very obvious that shortly, we would all be

transferred to England. In fact, the order came that all our families would be transferred to Northorn, together with husbands, wives and children, waiting for transport.

Before that, however, Christmas and New Year were approaching, our last in Germany. Our unit was invited to go to the port town, Wilhelmshaven, for a New Year's Eve ball. The captain of our unit, with a number of medals for bravery, was on duty that day. Therefore, he kindly lent me his uniform (not a good practice). We had a grand time at the ball. Jola was there too, of course (we had a nanny to look after Ingrid). We invited the New Year in for the last time in Germany, but in the Scottish tradition. This meant that all were drunk, and kisses were free! For the first time, I experienced what is meant by the traditional Scottish celebration.

When we returned home, and I remember this fact only from Jola, I was apparently very correct, thanking our German babysitter, but as soon as she was gone, I dropped half-dead on to the bed. I had a very bad headache the next morning!

On a lighter note, when our unit was moved to Lingen, Jola and Ingrid were still in Bawinkel. The order came that all army families must be transferred to Northorn. I was asked to take a three-ton lorry, completely loaded with steel bedsteads, and go to Northorn. I drove the lorry, and my passengers were a lieutenant of the unit, sitting beside me, and a sergeant with full equipment, who clambered on top of the bedsteads. The lorry was covered with a tarpaulin roof, and the distance we were to drive about was 170 kilometres. The lieutenant liked a fast ride; therefore, I was doing about sixty or seventy miles per hour.

People whom we were passing were waving at us;

these we interpreted as friendly gestures. I did not stop until I arrived at the barracks in Northorn. There we discovered to our horror that our interpretation of the enthusiasm of the bystanders was completely wrong. What had actually happened was that the tarpaulin roof had split into two along the middle of the lorry, and the poor sergeant had been constantly beaten by the flapping sides. You can imagine the reception he gave me!

During our last days in Northorn family quarters we were accommodated in a beautiful German villa. One evening, the wife of an officer went to have a bath. Suddenly we were woken up by the screams of that lady from the bathroom. Hearing the cries for help, her husband, hardly dressed, was first on the scene with a revolver in his hand. Seeing his wife shaking while standing in the bath and holding onto the metal chain to the light switch above, it was apparent that she was being electrocuted. He grabbed her by the other hand. Unfortunately, as he was standing barefoot on the tiled floor, he experienced an electric shock as well. By this time all the occupants of the villa, and there were many, some of them armed, stood speechless, at the doorway until a more practical man grabbed a walking stick, and pulled the chain away. There were endless talks about this incident in our canteens and quarters.

In a few more days' time, we boarded the channel ferry and crossed to Dover. The sea was very rough and almost everyone was seasick. Once in Dover, the British organised the reception committee on a magnificent scale, with nannies for the babies, and stretchers for the ill and poorly after the crossing. The customs control was almost waived to all the passengers, and we were immediately sent to have a day of rest in one of the London hotels. Our embarkation documents were signed and stamped with the date 22 February 1947.

I have to add a few points, which will clear my earlier and later statements.

Polish army units of the First Armoured Division under General Maczek were spread in several places in north-west Germany, after the initial invasion and occupation. If I remember rightly, the headquarters were in Aurich. The sanitary section was in Hazeltine, where our friend Dr Alik Domaradzki (whose story will be continued later about our life in England) was the divisional doctor.

One battalion of artillery was stationed at Bawinkel; that was where I belonged. Then another in Lingen, plus the famous Northorn, Wilhelmshaven, etc.

Our best friends at the time were, of course, Maryla and Tadzik Tworkowski, who had been married almost immediately after the allied invasion. Similarly, Henia and Alik Domaradzki (who had completed his medical studies just prior to the invasion, at Edinburgh University; he had begun his studies at the famous Warsaw Sanitary School, before the war) were married very soon after the German capitulation. Henia, Alik and their family have remained our very best friends, always ready to give their advice and help. They now live in Wolverhampton, where Alik is a very successful GP.

As I said earlier, there were five girls from the Oberlangen POW camp, closely kept with Jola, and they were first registered in Aurich military camp. From there they were moved to help to organise the life in Maczkow.

Ingrid, my daughter, was born on 5 July 1946. Jola's stay was extended to 26 February 1947 by the IV Polish Service Panza's transit camp in Northorn, Neuhausen BAOR.

Some of the girls, when living in Maczkow, were married, like Danusia Nowiak. I do not remember where Irene Zabiello came from, but I do remember that she had a daughter, Margaret, nearly the same age as Ingrid, and we helped each other very much in those rather difficult times in Germany.

There would of course be scores of other names, which came to mind later, of some of the girls from the DP camps, and the POW camp in Oberlangen. Many of them were quickly verified by the Underground Army, which had formed headquarters in Maczkow, and they were issued with a document that gave them status for their future life.

Some of the women and men travelled very quickly abroad to different countries, not setting their feet in England at all. Some returned to Poland, and some went to Italy, to join the second Polish corps, under General Anders. The latter arrived in England at a later stage, when the war with Germany was completely finished and the final surrender had been signed. Still in Italy, the Polish army organised courses for the young girls and boys. These courses allowed many of them to obtain matriculation status, or even some trade or profession, before they arrived in England.

Danusia Sujkowska, another friend, married later to Danek Francki and settling for a relatively short time in London. We have been very good friends. There was the family of Hanka Czarnocka; her mother was very much involved in the AK movement, and she was given very quickly a responsible job of building the archives of that organisation, for the period of the war. Hanka married Zbirochowski-Koscia, and they now live in London. There was also Halina Lausz and her husband, who for a short time, were good friends of ours.

Still in Germany, Ingrid, in 1946, had a German nanny. It was a very happy time, as the Fräulein came from a very good German family, was well educated, and according to German tradition she was attached to other families doing all their work, and thus getting used to the normal life.

There were a number of Polish officers who were also our friends. There were also some officers adopted by the Polish division from POW camps, like Lieutenant Fuchs, who was a very gun-happy man from the underground movement and Warsaw Uprising – for him to adapt to normal civilian life was almost an impossibility.

I have given this short résumé of the people who in some way affected our life after being liberated from the Germans, and before we decided to go to England. In this way, I hope this may enlarge your picture about us, and introduced some names that became a part of our life later.

As with all types of autobiographical books, one has to be extremely careful when quoting other people's names, and their whereabouts. I am fully aware that in this way, I may misrepresent relations, friends or even acquaintances, by not giving all the details of any happening, or by giving too many details. In fact, I cannot win.

Unfortunately, by substituting such names with fictitious ones, I would be ruining my work completely. It is not fiction; it must be factual, and giving my sincere apologies, I must risk the consequences.

Anyway, we are about to enter probably the most important time of my life. I hope the next chapter will prove even more interesting.

Life in London

Our names were eventually entered on to a list of the members of the Polish soldiers of BAOR, and their families who were allowed to enter the United Kingdom. The documents were issued on 22 February 1947.

As I described in the previous chapter, we stayed in the Polish Service Families Transit Camp in Northorn, waiting for orders for departure. However, on 25 September 1947, we arrived at the port of Harwich, in England.

From there Jola and Ingrid were transferred to the resettlement camp in Sherborne, Dorset. I, on the other hand, was moved to the military resettlement corp in Whitley, Surrey.

I went a few times to visit Jola, and we decided to accept the offer of a room with a little kitchen in a terrace house, owned by friends at 181 Holland Road, London. This house belonged to Barbara and Leszek Bachrynowski, who were known to us from our time in Germany. Unfortunately, they were not very popular in Germany; therefore, we realised that we were taking a great risk. Nevertheless, the alternatives at that time were almost non-existent. Therefore, as soon as it was possible, I arranged the transfer of Jola, Ingrid and our belongings to 181 Holland Road.

My memory fails me, and in this case, I can only give the approximate time when this happened. Most probably it was very late in 1947, say November or the beginning of

December. Jola stayed with Ingrid in the house alone for a very short time. She had many friends in London, who visited her very often with a helpful hand.

There were Mr and Mrs Bregman not far away, on the other side of the same street. There were Mr and Mrs Cumft, who were extremely helpful. There were Maryla and Tadzik Tworkowski, Henia and Alik Domar, the Koscia family, and many others. I used to come every weekend.

During one week, Mr Olgierd Cumft helped me with an interview at an engineering firm, Messrs Kleine Co. Ltd, where eventually I got my first job, on 7 January 1948, and was transferred from the resettlement corp to the reserve, if only for 279 days, ending on 13 October 1948.

This period of my – or our life – was extremely trying, and I would like to give it appropriate attention in my story.

The separation on arrival in the UK between Jola with the baby, and I, was not only painful to us, but also very obstructive in our efforts to organise our start for civilian life. Jola was living a kind of communal life in primitive barracks, while my existence in Whitley Camp was simple vegetation. Only through the good relationship with my commanding officer, who was very under-standing, did I manage to have many days off, by exchanging duties with others, in order that I could travel to Jola's camp, where she could be cherished and uplifted from her very depressive mood. This also enabled me to travel to London to look for possible accommodation and a job that would allow me to get the release from the resettlement corp, and enable us to start our life in this, to us, very strange country.

The initial task was very depressing for me, as I found

Jola constantly crying in desperation. We were in constant touch with friends in London, and with their help visualised the possibility of finding a solution to these pressing problems.

I don't remember how we got in touch with Leszek and Barbara Bachrynowski. I know that I had been in constant touch with him earlier, whilst still in Germany, and that he was released earlier than I, for the purpose of starting architectural studies in London. Therefore, both of them were soon released from the army. With the demob money, they managed to purchase the house in Holland Road, and after obtaining a government grant he started his studies. It was therefore clear that they were the obvious contact for us to make, where accommodation was concerned.

When the possibility of accommodation in the Bachrynowski house became real, we decided to accept it without even thinking of possible consequences. We thought that, for one pound and ten shillings a week, we could manage, especially once the possibility of my employment started to materialise. This was due to finding a vacancy in the paper, and to Olgierd Cumft taking me for an interview with the directors of the Kleine Co. Ltd, in George Street, London. You must remember that I did not know any English.

At that interview the director asked me whether I knew any German. 'Yes, of course,' was my reply. Then he said it would be no trouble because, in his own words, 'Our chief engineer, Mr Roche, knows that language too; he had been a major in the British army, in the Normandy action.'

I got the job, but as to the knowledge of German by Mr Roche, it was, as I would call it, 'girlfriend German', which was no help to me.

As I was employed as a draughtsman only, on six pounds per week, it appeared there would be no problem with the language. Actually, there were many, but more about them later.

Jola's move was arranged, and she landed with a host of problems in 181 Holland Road, but free at last. There were already problems with that move, but with the camp officials' help the whole thing was most satisfactorily arranged.

I will describe the accommodation. It consisted of one and a half rooms, in a semi basement, adjoining the shallow cellar under the front of the house. There was a small yard, surrounded by high walls. The whole row of houses on that side of Holland Road, boarded the Underground line. Incidentally, this house has now been demolished, and a new bypass road constructed in its place. There are not even the remains of the place where our life in London, England, began.

As I was saying, the flat let consisted of one and a half very small rooms, accessible by a few steps down from the ground floor corridor. There were two windows, looking into the fourteen-foot by eight-foot yard, which were hardly above ground level. The furniture (as it was let as a furnished flat) was almost non-existent. Therefore, our big trunks were the main wardrobe and cupboards. The only furniture consisted of a home-made double bed, and a little table with chairs. I think it was constructed ad hoc by Leszek himself. There was no mattress as such, but several coiled springs with a kind of canvas stretched across the top. There was a primitive sink (earthenware) and a little worktop. There was also a door from our room to the cellar. It was full of rubble, pitch-black, with rats, mice and all other vermin.

Jola arrived, with baby Ingrid, pram and our other belongings. It was extremely difficult for us to arrange all that. However, we were used to camp life and to war conditions, and Jola treated her predicament as an extension of that. The families of unemployed today are provided with superior conditions, as seen on television.

I was still in the camp in Whitley, and every weekend I would come to London to help her, and to discuss our future. Even when I was accepted for my first job, it took a few days for the different authorities to give me rights to work, and to be discharged from the resettlement corp into the state of reserve. Eventually, I started my work on 12 January 1948. I was still awaiting a document from the Home Office.

It would not be bad at this juncture to describe the situation of Polish people and probably other minorities and their families in England. There were probably 200,000 to 300,000 Poles, who 'invaded' this country. It does not matter that they had been defending this country during both the blitz, and later during the threat of invasion, and still much later during the invasion of France and Germany. After VE day, people tended to forget those facts. They only think that so many Poles, or Czechs or Hungarians or people from other Eastern countries have come here to benefit from the very meagre provisions this country had to offer, even to their own people, forgetting about the other people of the world. There was still rationing in England. The jobs were scarce, and there were the lucky Poles trying to grab the employment from their English counterparts. There was great reluctance to accept us. Not only this, but should there be a criminal offence by a Polish citizen, it would be in the headlines for days. No one would accept that, within our community, there were criminals too. It took us a long time to establish the fact that our community was not any worse than the English one.

Later on I used to hear the statements, 'What is so spectacular about Poles that they manage to occupy the key positions in our industries?' It took me a long time to explain that at the end of the 1939 invasion, only the cream of the Poles managed to escape to the West. They learnt the language and worked very hard to occupy the best positions, in both industry and, what is so interesting to me, engineering. They were, and still are, the best of the Poles.

Looking back, I realise now, how difficult it was for us to establish ourselves, and to prove that through hard work we were contributing to return this country to its pre-war greatness.

As I said earlier, we found many of our friends, most of them known to us still in Germany, some like the Cumft family, well known to Jola and her family from Warsaw. Many who travelled through Italy with the Polish Second Corp under the Polish leader General Anders. The Bregman family is one example. I have already mentioned that they lived on the opposite side of Holland Road.

Mr and Mrs Bregman and their daughter Barbara (another Barbara) knew Jola and her parents from the time in Warsaw. They were of Jewish descent, and Mrs Bregman and her daughter were imprisoned in the Jewish ghetto in Warsaw.

Mr Bregman was in the army at the start of the war in Poland. Nearing the total capitulation, many units converged towards the southern border, and via Romania escaped to the Middle East. There they were joined by a large contingent of ex-Polish soldiers and families, who had been taken prisoner by the Russians. This was done by the agreement between West and East, so that the Russians gave an amnesty to all Poles taken prisoner. All those Poles were eventually trained and organised into the so-called Second Corp. They formed, finally, the backbone of the invading Allied forces into Italy. Mr Bregman was then in charge of a supply unit, behind the front lines. I think he held the rank of major.

Meanwhile, Mrs Bregman and her daughter were, with the help of Jola's father, released from the ghetto. Later, at the end of the Warsaw Uprising, young Barbara walked out of Warsaw with the white handkerchief, surrendering herself as a civilian. I think this is something that will haunt her pride to the end of her life.

Somehow, at the end of the war, or very close to that moment, Mr Bregman managed, via the Polish/British military contacts, to bring his wife and daughter from Poland to Italy, the part of Italy which was already occupied by the Allied forces. There, Barbara went to school and matriculated, before arriving to England as part of the Second Corp, families.

After being demobilised, the Bregman family established themselves in Holland Road. Mr Bregman's brother, who at that time was editor of the *Polish Soldiers Daily* in London, lived with his wife in the Wembley area. Those two families were very well-off, but rather mean, even to themselves.

When Jola's mother arrived in London from Poland, they actually refused to recognise that they owed her anything besides a thank you. The fact that Jola's parents saved Mrs Bregman's and her daughter's lives was simply forgotten. Jola's mother and father spent large sums of money in securing their release from the Warsaw ghetto. They both stayed for a long time in Jola's flat, which was under constant surveillance by the SS units, because of Jola's work in the underground movement.

Their house was raided several times by the SS Gestapo, and each time both Mrs Bregman and Barbara hid either in the flat or in the loft space. Once, actually, Barbara had hidden herself under the eiderdown and blankets on the bed, and was not noticed by Gestapo soldiers.

In every such case, should they both have been discovered, the entire household would have been arrested and if not killed on the spot, then certainly sent to concentration camps.

The Bregmans, however, in 1955 would rather forget such incidents, even knowing how much Jola's mother suffered since the war, and how much of that suffering was due to her action in trying to save the Bregmans' family.

In London, Barbara was enrolled as soon as possible to the London School of Economics, and finished it quite well. She married a Mr Marlow, who added a new dimension to their life. They have two daughters: Monica and Joanna. The family became Roman Catholic whilst still in Poland.

Mrs Bregman died some years back, and when Mr Bregman was left on his own, he tried to be close to his daughter and grandchildren. So he sold his home in Holland Road and an extension was built on to the Marlows' house. After moving there, he became very isolated and unhappy, wandering by himself anywhere in London; he even managed to come to Ixworth to tell us his sad story. Later he died.

As I said earlier, on the first day of my employment, I realised that I had no means of communicating with my colleagues. I started, therefore, a book, in which daily I would register every single new word and its application. This helped me enormously. I had to learn the Imperial measuring system too. After six months, however, I could converse reasonably well. I was working some overtime, doing calculations of quantities. This was done in longhand/mentally. In this way, I have been very well introduced to the Imperial system, and I challenge any of the young men today to calculate mentally the simple volume of a concrete section (i.e. twelve and one-twelfths multiplied by seven and five-eighths multiplied by thirty-two and seven-sixteenths). Twice a week after office hours we would spend another one and a half hours on preparing such bills of quantities. For that work I would receive one pound and ten shillings, tax free, per week, which when added to my six pounds wages was quite an appreciable addition.

The staff were extremely helpful, and besides frequent funny stories, based mainly on my misunderstanding English expressions or using incorrect spelling, or more often mispronunciations, I was very happy there. Nearing the end of my employment with this company (3 December 1948), when I received very good references, I even attended the first annual dinner, which was held in a very large first floor room in one of Holborn's pubs. I suppose there were more than 120 employees (it was also a contractual firm), many of whom I already knew from visiting their building construction sites, to the north of the Holborn area.

I remember, that at this very jolly celebration, the secretary of the company, Mr Palmer, when challenged, got up and one by one, without any records, named every single man present. Incidentally, it was a 'men only' affair.

The firm originated in Germany and one of the two directors was of German descent, from the family of Mr Kleine, who established the firm in the early twenties in Germany. It was started by the introduction of Kleine floor construction, which I already knew of from my father's technical books.

Mr Roche, the chief engineer, with his deputy, started doing their private practice jobs, even in office hours, which was very bad indeed. Unfortunately, he was involved with some intermediary man who was managing his financial and business affairs; and when Mr Roche left the firm, this intermediary also left him penniless and in debt. Later I learnt that Mr Roche committed suicide.

I was also misguided when I left this firm, as I was advised that I should sit the university entrance examination in order to join the university. It was a great failure, as my knowledge of English was still not adequate for this purpose.

Meanwhile, Jola was struggling through her life on our meagre income. I must say, she managed quite well. Everything, including clothing, food, fruit and sweets, was all still rationed. This was helpful in a roundabout way, because the prices on ration coupons were controlled and kept very low.

We would entertain many of our friends despite our small resources; there could often be well over ten or even fifteen people in our small room. On such occasions, Ingrid, in her pram, which was covered well with the strong net to prevent mice from attacking her, was pushed into the cellar space. She would be quite good, not crying too much. I remember that during the first Christmas, when I was still in Whitley Camp, I managed to make for her a very large teddy. I used some blankets, flock from our discarded mattresses, and large army metal buttons for the eyes. When I brought this toy to our flat, Ingrid burst into tears – she was terrified. That was the end of the teddy. We eventually got her a small one, which she treasured for many years.

There were two other incidents in our first accommodation that I shall mention. London was, at the time, infested by the effects of incredibly fog, which used to be called a pea-souper. It was yellowish-brown in colour, and was a simply awful experience. The whole of London experienced this type of fog for many years, until the capital was made a smokeless zone; all open coal fires were banned and all factories, and power stations were ordered to put on their chimneys' special filters. I will tell stories about that fog later. Anyway, in those early days, especially spring and autumn, it was a great problem.

Once Jola was invaded by ever-complaining Barbara (nicknamed 'Major Barbara' by us), saying to Jola that because of her washing of nappies, the whole house was full of damp, with running water on all walls. Unsurprisingly, Jola did not appreciate that, knowing that this was the result of the fog, and not her washing.

The other incident was very funny indeed. I managed to construct shelves for some food, books and other various effects; they were made of timber parts and of 'cellotex' (fibre boards). As I have already explained, we had constant visits from the cellar by mice. They always managed to make new holes in the walls at floor level. When I sealed the previous holes, they would then climb over our shelves and consume the cellotex shelf material. It was disastrous, and I decided to put an end to it by catching one of the mice, and putting it into a little metal cage in front of the latest hole, hoping that it would inform its friends to go away. This I did by designing a lasso-loop to hang over the hole. I caught a mouse, the cage was already made, and the mouse was put in the cage pronto. Unfortunately, the result was the opposite to my expectation. Its friends took pity on it, and they arrived in groups, conglomerating around the cage. After parading this mouse on the lasso-like lead, I eventually got rid of it. I introduced poison instead. I did not know then that one could call the Health Inspector to organise the official eradication of vermin.

A little later, Maryla and Tadzik arrived from Scotland. Tadzik had finished a special course with Marconi on servicing television sets; this had been organised for him by the resettlement corp. He got a job in Boyd's factory in London, and they moved at first to a house further along Holland Road from us. Jola had some extra help and a great friend in Maryla. By this time, they had had their only child, a son named Andrew. We have been very close with them, and eventually Tadzik's mother, for many years.

They decided to move to Balham to a house owned by Mr Tabaczinski, a historian. The first floor of his house was let to many people, room by room. There were two rooms vacant, and Tadzik, Maryla and Andrew took the large corner room, whilst Jola, Ingrid and I got a smaller adjoining room. There were two other rooms occupied by coloured people (students), who were a married couple.

I must now briefly describe the situation. The

Tabaczinski family occupied the whole of the ground floor. As I said, he was a historian, specialising in ancient Greek, Roman and Egyptian history. To do his research he required a lot of peace in his study, which was mostly below the Tworkowskis' room. As the room was a very large one, even walking across would cause a lot of vibration. This was very much resented.

On our floor there was one bathroom, with incorporated toilet and a communal kitchen. With so many people, the toilet was a great problem – we even installed chairs for those having to wait. However, the more difficult part was the kitchen. The students from the West Indies cooked their traditional meals, which required many hours of boiling. This consisted of foods mixed with very strong spices, and the smell would spread over the whole of the first floor. It was almost completely unbearable, and there were occasions when Tadzik and I would be near to physical action. Somehow, we survived.

It was whilst living in Mr Tabaczniski's house, at 89 Ramsden Road, Balham, that we decided to have our first holiday in Britain.

In either 1948 or 1949, Jola and I decided to have one week's holiday on the Thames (perhaps you have read *Three Men in a Boat*, by Jerome K Jerome). We purchased a large inflatable dinghy in a government surplus store, which could easily accommodate the two of us plus our luggage. We also took with us a small tent, which we intended to erect over the inverted dinghy. There was a special pump and an emergency kit supplied.

Firstly, we decided to have a trial run (or should I say, a trial row), therefore, we took the dinghy by bus to the famous Cheyne Walk, close to Battersea Bridge. As there appeared to be no one in sight, we went down the steps to the small landing area. I inflated the dinghy, which had two seats and a set of oars that had to be threaded through special loops. We located ourselves correctly, and started to row. At first it was fine and only by one of the piers of Battersea Bridge there appeared to be some weirs, which made our navigation rather precarious. Nevertheless, we returned safely to our base. I deflated the dinghy, packed it into the bag and we departed.

There was one small problem – we were completely drenched. Consequently, when the bus arrived, we managed very quickly to occupy the seats behind the driver. We paid our fares to the totally unaware conductor, and then we realised that our seats were becoming more and more saturated. It was like sitting on a sponge. On our arrival to Balham, as quickly as we could, we ran off the bus and home.

We learnt later on that our little experience on the Thames was very dangerous indeed, and we should not have been allowed to have our little row, as many people had apparently drowned in this area.

Our holiday was a little nightmarish, but we enjoyed it anyway. It took us six days and five nights to travel from Reading Park to the Windsor area. We had to negotiate numerous locks. The people who saw us thought we were absolutely mad, and any pleasure boat we encountered jostled us like we were a little shell. It didn't matter, even when on the last day, when getting out on a high bank, Jola got out but I lost my balance and the boat, with its entire contents, tipped over. The river at that point was about six-foot deep, but we managed to fish out nearly all of our possessions. The document of this expedition was the guidebook, fully saturated with water! It was good to be young and adventurous, and I would challenge anyone to do the same today. The guidebook was dried out and is still in our bookcase.

During that holiday there were many incidents, and it would be difficult to give details of all of them. But one or two, might throw some light on this week, about how bizarre it was for two relatively young people to embark on such an adventure.

First of all, after our trial run, we packed carefully the minimum of necessary items, clothes and food for the week. That meant, of course, a Primus stove. Then we packed them into water-proof bags, together with the dinghy, its little oars and the tent, then we caught a Green Line coach to Reading.

When we arrived in Reading, we went to have coffee and cake, the last for a week in civilised conditions, and we started to look for a place from where we could cast off our dinghy. We saw a park along the Thames, and there we went. We pumped up the dinghy, loaded our belongings, and when we were almost ready to push it into the water we saw a park keeper shouting in the distance and waving a stick. I said to Jola, 'Come on, we have to be quick now.' Before he reached us, we were already waving to him, as we were fifteen or twenty foot away from the bank.

After passing through many locks, we started to look for a mooring and camping place. Unfortunately, it was almost impossible to find such places. We managed to find somewhere where there was a very small area, and there we stopped.

Here I have to explain that the dinghy, when turned upside down, was to act as our bed. The luggage was stored under this 'bed' for safety, and the tent erected above it. Some blankets, a couple of sheets and pillows, and a hot-water bottle completed the arrangements. So the first night came and passed without any serious incidents.

The penultimate night of our holiday we had to spend on a small island. It was completely overgrown with all kinds of wild plants and bushes. I had to chop some back to arrange a little clearing for our camping. In the distance we saw on either side of what was by now, quite a wide river, very impressive mansions with huge gardens, each with various boats anchored to private landing stages.

We then realised that, one thing we had forgotten to replenish, was the fresh water can. Therefore, Jola rowed the empty dinghy to one of those well-off places. She disappeared for quite a long time, returning when darkness had already fallen. Apparently, she had been invited for a cup of tea by the only occupant of one of the large estates, a rather old Lady with a title, butler and a beautiful house. She wanted to invite us for the night, but Jola refused, and quite rightly too. It was our holiday, which was to remind us of our camping days in Poland. We were a little worried about snakes and such intruders as water rats, but after a hot meal and a little bonfire, we enjoyed the evening and, rather tired, had a good night's sleep.

In the morning, reluctantly, we went away for the last stay near Windsor, where we had the accident that I mentioned at the beginning, with the overturned dinghy. From Windsor, we took another Green Line coach, and back to Ramsden Road. We were very tired, but pleased with ourselves. Whatever other people were saying, we considered our little escapade to be a great success.

One light-hearted moment was when one day I purchased in an old second-hand shop an old-fashioned gramophone and two records. They were, I remember well, the record of Amelita Galli-Curci: The 'One Fine Day' aria from *Madame Butterfly*, and *Peer Gynt's* 'Morning' by Greig. They were great fun, and we played them many times. I think I paid less than ten shillings, or fifty pence in today's money, for the whole thing.

It was at the suggestion of Halina and Olgierd Cumft that for a short time, we moved to their house at 77 Eaton Place, Belgravia; this was 1 March 1949. They had realised our predicament of living in Balham.

I must say here a few words about the Cumft family. Olgierd Cumft had been a pilot in the Polish air force before war broke out in 1939. Some time in the beginning of 1938 he had a very bad crash in a monoplane. This resulted in him being assumed dead; his body was transferred to the mortuary, and it was only when visited by his friend, who very fortunately noticed Olgierd Cumft's eye blinking, that they realised he was alive. He notified the military hospital, and Olgierd was immediately transferred there. He was unconscious for almost a whole year. After that he recovered fully apart from a muscle in his right shoulder. This would not respond to any treatment, becoming an almost permanent wound.

However, the Polish authorities, in recognition of his military service, offered him and his wife the post of Military Attaché in Manchuria.

There, the unbelievable happened. He was sent to a doctor (who had dismissed the awarded diploma he had received at St Petersburg) who had begun to do what we would nowadays call a 'healing' service. He would take a handful of mineral crystals and ask the patient to blow on them. Then, looking into his patient's eyes, and at the crystals, he would reveal the main problem which he believed the patient to be suffering from.

Apparently, he did not know anything about Mr Cumft; however, he described fully what had happened to him and what his problem was, in that the wound of the missing muscle would not heal. He prescribed to Mr Cumft an ointment that was made from Manchurian tiger's whiskers. To the great surprise of everyone, the wound healed. That was in 1940 – penicillin or other antibiotics were not yet known.

By now, scientists have discovered that the roots of Manchurian tiger's whiskers are embedded in the glands that contained a substance very similar to penicillin. This substance would help the tiger to heal it after being wounded.

I personally thought that this story was so fascinating, that I started to treat most of the 'healers', especially those from the Far East, with much greater respect. You must therefore forgive me for this small digression!

Olgierd Cumft had the rank of Squadron Leader whilst still in Poland. He was a friend of Jola's family, and that is why he managed to find us in Germany. In London, he helped me to find and secure my first job, and now he and Halina took pity on us, and offered to share their small flat with us, until such time as we would be more successful in finding better accommodation.

I must now add that of the Cumft family, only two of them arrived in England during the war. They arrived via Japan, South Africa and the USA. That was certainly due to his diplomatic career. In London, they were offered a house in the most desirable location, Eaton Place, Belgravia.

We had several very pleasant months whilst living with them. It was a bit of a squash, but I think we all enjoyed our life there with lots of smiles and funny moments. Not everyone would believe that we were living at 77 Eaton Place. The eyebrows were raised in many quarters. For those who do not know, Belgravia, where Eaton Place is situated, had been requisitioned during the war by the British authorities for many illustrious figures from different nations who were simply homeless, due to Hitler's action.

On the other hand, some of the large but much simpler buildings were given to house the homeless children. There were several ambassadors, even the Polish President in exile, who resided three houses away from us, with a soldier on duty, a pre-war flag displayed and the full diplomatic protocol followed.

The houses were not very big and were mostly Victorian. The only visit to London paid by Chopin, where he played only one concert, was four houses away in the opposite direction to our President. (There is a plaque on the wall of the house where Chopin played, and the piano was not used by anyone else.) Belgravia is centrally placed to Harrods, Hyde Park, Pall Mall and, if your position is high enough, close to Buckingham Palace.

During our life at Eaton Place, we managed to go for a day to Brighton. It was a very hot summer Sunday, and we got so sunburnt that for a day or two, we had to go to bed completely naked. This was, as we found later, to the great delight of the watchful eyes of the people on the other side of the rear yard. Thus we discovered that one has to draw the curtains to enjoy one's privacy. We did not want to be called exhibitionists!

It was again with the help of Olgierd Cumft that we managed to get a flat in Milton Chambers, 128, Cheyne Walk. This we rented from London and Westcliffe Properties Ltd, and we moved there on 28 September 1949. Probably to the great relief of the Cumft family. Nevertheless, we were extremely grateful for their help.

In Cheyne Walk (near the Whistler beach), we were firstly on the second floor, and then later we moved to the ground floor. We stayed in this flat for a considerable time.

I started work again after the fiasco of my studies. My next job was in Sunbury, Surrey; I was there between February 1950 and May 1951. I travelled every day from Clapham Junction to Sunbury in an empty train, as most of the London commuters would be travelling in the opposite direction. Square Grip, as the firm was called, was a very interesting small company. The managing director was a mechanical engineer, who had designed and developed a brilliant idea. He realised that if a square section of mild steel bars could be twisted along its length to a certain number of twists, the crystalline of the steel would change, converting the mild steel bar into a high tensile one, with the strength 50 per cent higher. The design of such machinery was extremely difficult, but he managed to produce motors for the bars up to ten inches thick. At the same time, he also designed a special method of producing mesh of such twisted bars, naturally small in sections, and used them in factory concrete floors.

It must be emphasised at this juncture, that reinforced concrete in Britain in the thirties and even through to the early fifties, was very much behind American and European progress. Those of South America were especially very much in the foreground. For that reason, Square Grip Reinforcement Ltd allocated a sum of well over £2,000 per year for establishing a laboratory for the development in the field of reinforced concrete.

The reason for the lack of progress in this field of engineering was two-fold. Firstly, as the English architects were mostly artists, and also they developed their skills from master builders, their structural engineering was almost non-existent. You could actually, before 1950, become a structural engineer just by paying a minimum fee of £100. I do not remember when the structural engineers received their Royal Charter, but it was much later, and the position of structural engineers was helped by those engineers who came to England, mostly of Jewish origin, escaping Hitler's regime from 1936 onwards.

Oscar Faber, Freshman, Hajnal-Konyi and many others came to this country and helped to give status to structural engineering. They helped people like Manning and Reynolds to start competing with the continent, with people like Le Corbusier, Nervi, Cantello and others, who were trained in both branches of architecture and structural engineering. These men had designed very impressive buildings, both housing and exhibition halls, and these were copied here in Britain.

Our life in Chelsea, 128 Cheyne Walk, Milton Chambers, was a real eye-opener to life in London or even Britain. Chelsea was an extension of the West End. Probably we would call it a mixture of second grade and of wealthy West-Enders, with a deep tradition of the young avant-garde, of rich and not so rich, even to the very poor.

Our best friend Cumft trained as a watchmaker, and

we witnessed one day the opening of his watch repair shop in Walton Street. It was, so to speak, the borderline between Knightsbridge and Chelsea. It was in the time when the tax office officers were your friends. They actually went to him to advise him on how to arrange the accounts, even how to spread the bills, for spending on furnishings, decorating and supplying his shop over two or three years, in order that his business would begin with some credit in those early difficult years, and not be straight away in the red. He needed this help very badly, as I will explain!

Some of his customers were, as I would call them 'ordinary' people; they were very good customers and always paid on the dot. These customers he needed very badly. There were also the 'aristocracy' – Lord So and So, etc. There were the people who married in nearby St Paul's, where all the society weddings would take place. On the other hand, they were on the financial decline. The result was that they would ring Olgierd Cumft and ask him to call at their house to repair their family heirloom, such as a grandfather clock.

Mr Cumft, with difficulty, collected this item, and perhaps one or two more, and within a week the clocks were returned, repaired and working beautifully, and he left his bill. After a lot of patience, and several telephone calls, Mr Cumft eventually received a cheque for his work. When he paid this cheque into the bank, it automatically bounced.

After a visit to the bank, Mr Cumft was enlightened by the manager that most of the local, declining 'nobility' would always have two accounts, one with money, and the other without money. It was his very good lesson, as he was never paid for that bill. Somehow, he had to keep his good reputation and manners in such a way that the money would arrive before the goods left his shop. Apparently even Harrods had the same problem.

I mentioned St Paul's – I must, however, add that the receptions for most of such weddings were held at Cheyne Walk, not far away from where we lived. I think it was the last house, opposite the houseboats almost at the edge of Battersea Bridge. Once, I remember, we noticed a colossal attraction; part of a film was being made on that part of the river. It was at night; the arc lights were over the whole area, even on the bridge, there were scores of technicians, film equipment and a number of stooges. Directors, producers and, of course, dozens of spectators. The poor boy who was thrown into the Thames had to repeat his part several times. We never saw the film, but it was great fun.

Chelsea, of course, was famous for its eccentrics. You could find them everywhere, and in those days they were completely harmless. Perhaps they offended the more prudent because of their behaviour or dress, but for others, it was a way of relieving their doldrums, to have fun at other people's expense. And the 'others' didn't mind. Perhaps because of that, King's Road, the main artery of Chelsea, was developing into something extraordinary. From Sloane Square to World's End, which was the nearest to us, this street was full of trendy shops where you could spend lots of money on styling your hair, buying a new dress or shoes. It was the predecessor of Carnaby Street.

On the other hand, you could start with World's End, with a couple of pubs, very busy bus stops and also busy stalls, with all sorts of jellied eels, cockles, pickled onions, vinegar and mustard, all on ice; whether in summer or winter. Some people would carry their pints from the pub and enjoy the fishy snacks. The smell was unbelievable! Further along King's Road, there were the so-called 'antique' shops, it was a very curious area. People from all walks of life would go there in search of hidden treasures. I personally liked that area, but I don't think I ever bought anything.

A little further towards Fulham, there was Walham Green market, a long street with dozens and dozens of fruit and vegetable stalls. We often used to do our shopping there. There were always interesting shops along this street – some must have been very old, almost Dickensian.

I was told that this was the only market in London where the local authority, by tradition, would subsidise the traders. That was why the fruit and vegetables were cheaper than anywhere else.

But returning to Cheyne Walk, one must not forget Stamford Bridge football grounds. Every Saturday from 2 p.m. until late at night, our street, which was the main link from the east and south of London, was packed with crowds in the happiest mood, converging towards the Chelsea grounds. In the evening, sometimes not so happy, they would return home. There were cars, coaches, minibuses and pedestrians, thousands of them. Opposite our front windows and adjoining the river wall were situated, I think, the only urinals in England of the French type. Circularly arranged walls of sheet metal with similar roof, with the space from ground to knee level. There was a similar space at the eaves. On Saturdays that place was fully occupied. Even coaches at night would stop, for the benefit of their passengers. It was horrible. The whole area was very bad and smelly indeed.

Very close to us, adjoining those urinals, was the main depot for the waste disposal unit, loading the rubbish on barges, and disposing of this, probably towards Pitsea near Southend. In summer it was simply terrible when the rubbish was left for the weekend unattended. The stench was unbearable. Then, further along this road, was Lott's Power Station. At that time, one of two provided the electricity for half of the Underground trains.

I had an assignment in this antiquated building, and remember the huge coal-fired boilers, supplied manually by about twelve men. The working conditions were extremely bad. On the other side of the river, were two factories, one chemical, and the other called Waste Paper Disposal, with a large banner announcing the fact that 1,000 tons of paper was wasted every week!

Behind all this was the most famous building of all, Battersea Power Station, with its four huge brick chimneys. The outlet at the top of each chimney was four foot in diameter. This power station is now under a preservation order – it is part of our heritage.

All these listed buildings added to the smelly 'comfort' in Cheyne Walk.

We had some added attractions after the 1951 Exhibition – the Battersea Festival Gardens. It was for years a great attraction, with Albert Bridge always fully decorated and beautifully painted. It is a very lovely bridge, never designed to carry all the traffic that it did. I don't know how many people know this, but that when the army was walking over that bridge, the order would be given for a free step – they were not allowed to walk in step, as this would endanger the bridge by inducing a swaying action.

When I was talking about the river wall earlier, I have to stress how important it is. It used to be called a sea wall, and in fact it serves as such. The level of the Thames, until the recently-built new flood barriers in the area of the old London docks, was subject to tide fluctuation.

Twice a day the tidal water would reach the first defence, Teddington Lock, and of course the houseboats opposite our house would either be afloat or resting on the river bed, leaning badly. One year the spring tide was at its worst, and it was only thanks to this wall that London was not flooded.

One night we were woken up by guards walking along our street, ringing large handbells and asking people to move out of their basement flats. This wall was then strengthened and increased in height to prevent a repetition of what happened.

Again, I do not know whether you are aware that London is sinking down at a rate of one foot per hundred years. Therefore, even the present defences will not last. It was predicted that if the flooding of London occurred, almost 50 per cent of its area would be covered with water. What a thought. All Underground tubes have special gates on either side of the Thames, to prevent water spreading should the tunnel under the Thames collapse, but this would not prevent ordinary flooding. Anyway, it was frightening when looking through the windows; we saw the houseboats floating at the top edge of the embankment wall. We were a proverbial whisker away from disaster.

One more thing connected with the houseboats was that there were wooden planks connecting all of them, forming a sort of path. These would be used by the owners, the postmen and milkmen. Dustbins lined the edge by the entrance, almost at the boundary of the waste disposal area described earlier.

I always admired the milkmen, carrying crates full of milk bottles along this shaky path, summer or winter, but especially during the latter as it was very risky indeed.

Some of the houseboats were extremely well equipped with cookers, washing machines, television sets, hi-fi equipment, etc. Some of them were more expensive than a detached house. However, you had to like such a style of life.

One could say a lot about the bad points of Chelsea life. However, I must add something that was not linked with Chelsea but with the whole of south London, or even part of central London. It was, of course, the famous fog (pea-souper, as it used to be called). I have already described some moments linked with the fog, when we were living in Holland Road. There are, of course, thousands of stories and jokes linked with this subject. I will therefore tell you only one or two. The Embankment, Cheyne Walk and Battersea were the worst places. Firstly, because they were the lowland areas of London, by the river and secondly, because of the industries that were conglomerated there, especially along the south bank of the Thames. I have already described some of them. Autumn and spring were the worst times of the year. During the winter there was a freezing variety of fog, which was treacherous.

The worst aspect of the days when such fog dominated London was that you tended to lose completely your sense of direction. I would walk out of our home in Cheyne Walk and I would not even be able to cross the road, always tending to return to where I started. The street lamps would hardly be visible.

Once, when taking a friend home to Battersea, we had to stop at the road crossing, and by touch read the names of the streets. Fortunately, in London, all street names were indented on the steel plates, so that you could read each name as though using Braille.

When Ingrid was just a little past one year old, Jola was pushing her in a small pushchair; she said that it was the worst experience for her to lose sight of Ingrid suddenly, because the fog was so thick. Besides the density of it, I think it was the effect on the eyes and on the breathing which was so horrible. Fortunately, one year later, the government announced that London would be a smokeless zone. All coal fires were banned, all factories were ordered to place special filters to their chimneys – and it worked. I would like, however, to finish with two rather light-hearted situations.

When working for Twisteel Co., I had to cross through Hyde Park every evening on my return to Chelsea. Hyde Park was, and is, infamous for its women of easy virtue. It was bad enough during dark autumn evenings to walk through the Park Lane area of Hyde Park, but during the fog, one could hear screams and laughter, and not be able to see anything, unless one got lost and tripped over such subjects. This resulted in endless jokes in the office the next day – when one would tell, with normal exaggeration, picturesque stories. Which brings me to another funny story.

We always used to take a stroll at lunchtime along Park Lane, or into Hyde Park. On one occasion, when walking with two of my friends, one of them, stepping over the kerb, noticed something lying in the gutter. He picked it up; it was a most beautiful lady's watch, with a gold bracelet decorated with diamonds. It was still working. We decided to take it to the local police station. To our surprise, the duty officer immediately called an expert, who apparently was there on most Mondays. He put a value of over £2,000 on the watch, took my colleague's name and address, and told him to call for it in a week's time. In any event there would be a 10 per cent reward for him. He called at the station a week later, and was told that no one had enquired about the watch. The police would keep it for a further month at which point, if not claimed, half of its value would be his, and after three months it would belong to him completely if it had not been claimed.

The police officer told us that there was such a colossal number of valuables brought into their station that they simply could not cope with them, especially on Mondays. That was the reason for the valuer and also the reason that they would not keep it in their safe. He told us that seldom did anyone claim a lost item, however valuable it was. After all, the embarrassment, should the husband (or wife) find what their partner had been doing over the weekend, would be much too great. The police officer told us that the whole length of Park Lane from Oxford Street, to Grosvenor House, was full of extremely luxurious pieds-à-terre.

Lastly, on the subject of fog, especially for the benefit of American visitors or any others, there was a little shop in Piccadilly Circus selling all sorts of souvenirs, where you could buy a small tin, well sealed with the inscription, 'The Famous London Fog'. Nobody would dare to open this tin, but business was always brisk for that item.

We were still in Cheyne Walk. Jola was at first working with Bateman Cleaners in King's Road. There she learnt how to lift up ladders in stockings by using an electric machine manufactured by 'Vitos'. There were as yet no tights, and ladder-proof stockings had not yet been invented. However, being already pregnant with Olgierd, the process of walking to the shop and back, and also the problems with Ingrid, were altogether too great for her. As a result we purchased this machine, and Jola started her job at home. We had an agent who brought the dirty stockings, and she would carry out repairs of up to fifteen ladders per stocking. This job was killing for her, but she persevered for quite a long time, day after day, week after week, until Olgierd was born. Then a little later, when we decided that enough was enough, we sold the machine, and I was extremely pleased to tell Jola not to look at laddered stockings any more.

Olgierd was born on 17 April 1950. I had taken Jola to St Stephen's Hospital in an ambulance three days earlier. It was very difficult for her to bring Olgierd into the world. Everyone was very happy to see him, even if we knew how difficult the first year of his life was to be.

Olgierd was crying every night; he tired his parents so much because we would get up several times every night just to turn him round. We would be doing it like automatons, sometimes in not agreed turns, or whoever would wake up first. Did I say the whole year? No, I was wrong, because for one night I pushed him across London to Portobello Road, where our friend Irene lived, who had offered to have Olgierd for one night. I don't know whether it was worth the effort. It was probably four miles there and four miles back, pushing the pram along undulating terrain of London. As far as I remember, Irene said she slept well!

There is a little story attached to the episode of Jola giving birth to Olgierd. As I was saying at the beginning of Olgierd's story, I was in the ambulance, taking Jola to the hospital, where after putting her to bed, it was decided by the doctor that it might take some time before Jola would give birth, and therefore I was advised to return home. The distance was not a problem, as it was quite close.

It was nearly midnight. I had taken Jola's possessions, including fur coat and all her underwear, and I proceeded to Cheyne Walk. I was stopped by the policeman on the beat, who asked me why I had ladies' clothing under my arm at that time of night. After a long explanation, he took upon himself to escort me to Cheyne Walk, where he wished me good luck and departed.

I was very dismayed at that time, because Mrs Bregman telephoned the hospital early in the morning and, learning of Olgierd's birth, which had been at fifteen minutes before midnight, this information was given to me by telephone second-hand, at my office. Now I think such things are well forgotten.

When Ingrid was very small, and Jola was working very hard, we learnt of a nursery that was run by two spinsters, one of whom was called Miss Welch, who was in charge. The nursery was especially for children of Polish parents, and was in Reigate, Surrey. Ingrid, together with Malgosia Zabiello, whom we knew still from Germany, stayed at the nursery, for a year or so. We travelled there by the famous London Green Line buses, once a week. We would visit Ingrid, and four years later her younger brother, Olgierd, for a few hours. Despite the fact that the nursery was excellent, it was very hard for us when each time we had to leave Ingrid for another week. Irena Zabiello was a good mother too, and many times travelled with us to Reigate.

Time was moving very fast indeed, and so the happenings affected our life so much so, that it is very difficult to build some continuity in my and our life.

Whilst we were still living in Cheyne Walk, Ingrid started school at the local Park Walk Primary School. She was sent home twice because of the presence of lice in her hair. We even had visits from the Health Inspector, who did not realise that lice preferred clean hair. Nevertheless, we had routine house inspections, but with the help of our family doctor, Dr Bernacinski, who was extremely good to us, such visits stopped.

Almost at the same time, we got to know Wiesiek Pilawski and Grace. He was an artist/painter, and as such he would of course have to live in Chelsea. Their first home was two streets away from Cheyne Walk. Grace was in the process of getting a divorce from her Scottish husband of the Campbell family.

Wiesiek, was having the same problem too, getting a divorce from his wife in Poland. However, he was an ardent Catholic, and therefore even when obtaining a divorce, he bluntly refused to enter into a second marriage. So his poor common law wife Grace, after his sudden death, was left with over 1,000 unframed paintings in her home and virtually nothing else. My children and I have paintings dedicated to us by him; he somehow valued my opinion about his work. This made me very proud. He had a great ability to go through the second-hand shops, buying lovely old frames, restoring them and adjusting them to suit his paintings.

Jola and I went to his one-man exhibition at the Wilton Gallery, Knightsbridge; it was a very respected place. He also exhibited in the Royal Academy, and was a member of the Royal Portrait Painters. Unfortunately, he drank rather a lot. His younger brother, who came twice from Poland, always brought as many spirits as possible.

The third time when he came, it was a very sorry story, as he came to collect and take his brother's ashes to Poland. He apparently had a great problem with the Customs Office. Jola and I visited Wiesiek's tomb in Warsaw Cemetery in 1976.

Grace remarried soon after his death to a very rich man, but unfortunately, after a year or two she died of cancer. It was a tragic life of a very promising young artist, as Grace was.

One light-hearted reminder was the little collie dog, which Wiesiek named (to tax Grace's vocal abilities) *Pszczolka* – which means 'little bee'. It was very cruel for Grace to have to pronounce the dog's name, especially as she used to exercise the dog on Camberwell Green and often had to call her loudly back.

Grace used to visit us often in Cheyne Walk, and it was she who said that we must do something for Ingrid's education, as in Park Walk School she was speaking and picking up very bad English. We took her advice, and with colossal effort, sent her to La Sagesse Convent School in Golders Green, London. Ingrid entered this school in September 1952. She stayed there for the whole preparatory year, and obtained very good testimonials from the Reverend Mother Gabrielle, BA. I still think it was very worthwhile to spend all that money and effort to give Ingrid a good start in life. She looked very lovely in her school uniform.

Wiesiek was a very good painter; he used to paint old Polish folklore scenes very well. In England, he loved to paint the sea; he especially loved Brixham Port, and he painted many pictures there. For his portraits, especially of Grace, he was admitted to the London Portrait Gallery, as a full member. For a short time he taught art in a private school for older girls in north London. It was a very lucrative job, but he hated to teach people without any talent, but with a lot of money.

We both influenced each other in our different artistic styles. He studied a lot in his early days and definitely possessed a gift. I certainly have a gift, but no training. Actually, I did have some small introduction whilst I was still in Poland, by my father's friend, a painter by the name of Parendyk and later by a third year student of Warsaw Polytechnic, who worked for my father. He studied architecture, and he taught me the rudiments of painting.

However, in Cheyne Walk, influenced by the memory of the great Whistler (it was actually called Whistler beach), and also by Wiesiek, but mostly because I was suffering from chickenpox, I took to painting watercolours. I had two dreadful weeks at home, during one of the hottest summers. Then, being in isolation, I simply looked through our window and painted many views of the Thames, Battersea and Chelsea Bridge, and many abstract objects. I must say, this sudden inspiration shook Wiesiek, the professional painter. After that he often asked for my opinion of his work. Unfortunately, he started searching for new ideas and there was no way of persuading him otherwise. That, quite frankly, ruined his prospects. He would be painting one subject in no less than twenty or thirty canvases, with some rather futuristic ideas. He was a post-impressionist, and perhaps if his life had been spared, he might have emerged as a completely new interpreter, like Cezanne, whom he admired greatly among many others.

Still on the subject of art... In Cheyne Walk, our ground floor flat was too big for us. Also, because of the shortage of our combined income, we let one room. One of our tenants was a student of law; he was with us for only a short time. The other was an Australian student of art, a sculptor. He was a very good tenant, and there would have been no problem with him living with us, but for one reason – he started creating his sculpture at home. He started developing a kind of reinforced concrete construction. The more appropriate name to it would be ferroconcrete; it was cement mixed with a small proportion of fine sand and water, and reinforced with lots and lots of fine wire mesh, which was easily shaped.

The idea was not new, as I was saying much earlier: there were good engineers and architects on the continent who used it. Mr Nervi, the Italian, designed most of the Olympic stadium and many other monumental structures, like the famous air terminal in Rome, plus a number of sailing boats, large and small, in the same type of ferroconcrete. Such concrete was extremely strong, light and elastic.

However, our young sculptor had gone too far; his sculptures were becoming monumental in both size and weight, and because of that, they had to remain in our house, as our doors were too small. Unfortunately, he had to demolish his perhaps very artistic designs, and we had to part with him.

When we moved from the second floor in Cheyne Walk, Mr and Mrs Bochdanowicz moved in. Halina was aged forty, he was somewhat older. I don't know, or simply don't remember their history, all I can say is that Halina was a very eloquent lady – she knew a number of languages and used to work as a secretary, a high-class international position. Her husband, as I knew him, was an upholsterer, and he even did some work for us. Halina had her mother, who lived until late years, and worked very hard on their household, almost to the last days of her life. To me she was a very celebrated woman.

Two years later, when we moved twice again, to Sunderland Road, in south London, they moved very close to us in Forest Hill. There, Halina, after some success, educated her boys in a very sophisticated way.

Antos, probably three years old by that time, would look through the window and say, 'I have just seen Mr Confucius.'

He also had an awful accident when walking upstairs one time. He simply went straight through the half-landing window, and on to the concrete footpath below – but there were no ill consequences! Once, I remember, all three boys went across the road to the garage of a rich man, and almost dismantled his car. They were educated extremely well from a Catholic point of view, but except for some Christmas cards, we eventually lost contact.

As I have said, Chelsea was famous for eccentrics. It was quite normal at the hours of 5 to 9 p.m. to see pairs in nightdresses walking along the embankment, or to see, as I remember it well, a sergeant wearing an unbuttoned battle-dress jacket, directing himself briskly towards Battersea (he was, I hasten to add, also wearing his trousers). It remains for me to say that on my daily walk to the office at Lower Grosvenor Street, which took me across Hyde Park, I would see several very elegant gentlemen (with bowler hats and umbrellas), who would exercise at a brisk march, or even run, in shorts, jumping over every single bench. At first, I thought they must be raving maniacs, but later I learnt that this was the fashion in the late forties and early fifties. Apparently, every decade has its own attractions.

I mentioned earlier that Irene helped us with Olgierd. It would not be out of place to say a few words more about her and her family. I have already mentioned Irene's daughter Malgosia in Germany. Malgosia was of a similar age to Ingrid, and we used to see each other for many years in London too.

Irene was divorced, and we learnt that she eventually married Janek Strauch, and soon after they had a new arrival in their son, Jacek. Janek was much older than Irene, and unfortunately finished his life much too early.

I remember their large leased flat, in the street close to Portobello Road in west London. It was much too big for them; therefore, they let part of it to different tenants. They both smoked like chimneys. They had to bring up their two children, and the lease of the flat was expiring very quickly. One has to remember that by law, you have to bring the house or flat to the same order as it was in when you bought the lease.

I must say I played a little trick on them, which was eventually quite beneficial to their future. I asked them where they would like to live, and they replied 'Middlesex'. I went to the head office of the estate agents in central London, and obtained the list of most of the firms operating in the Middlesex area. I sent to each of them identical letters requesting particulars of houses which I thought would suit the Strauch family. I posted those letters in one day – you can imagine how the replies were being pushed through their letterbox. There were virtually hundreds of them. Nevertheless, they bought a nice house and lived there very happily, except for the illness and death of Janek.

We kept constant contact with the Cumft family, especially when his shop was open, we visited him often.

Ingrid spent a lot of time with them in their flat. She was very talkative, and used to tell many improbable stories about how cruel we had been to her. At first, she was taken seriously by some of our friends, and it was only because of quick action on our part that the whole thing was eventually changed into a great laugh. Thank goodness for that.

All that time we were in touch with the Tworkowski family, and learnt that Tadzik had changed his job. Soon afterwards he got his place in Harrods, where he became known and highly valued as a salesman. Even today, he and his wife are highly valued for their work. Maryla established herself as chief accountant. She also found a niche for her daughter-in-law, Anka, to be trained for a similar post. Anka, who had married Andrew a few years back, learnt both English and the procedure for her job extremely quickly, gaining for herself quite a good position in Harrods. They have a daughter, Caroline, and a house in Tooting Broadway.

Tadzik's mother frequented Brixton Market at first, from where she accumulated numerous items of second-hand garments, to the dismay of her daughter-in-law. She would also have to step down from the pedestal of importance, which I described earlier. By this time she had isolated herself from the community. Now she has been placed in a home for elderly or mentally infirm people.

We have to admire the Tworkowski family, first of all because they live, even now, in the Stockwell block of flats, and that is after almost forty years. If you had seen those flats, you would understand my admiration. The Brixton area is about half mile away, similarly Clapham Common is not much further away, and of course

Stockwell itself is not much better, with its multiracial problems. These have been only too well highlighted in recent years. But of course, there are advantages; the Underground and network of buses are a stone's throw away. When the Victoria Line was built, it was more convenient to travel to the West End. So much so, that even their son Andrew and his wife Anka, bought eventually the house in Tooting, though he works as a lecturer in St Mary's College, East London. Andrew said that he works every morning on the train, and in the evening he reads the newspaper on his journey.

Maryla and Tadzik are of course on the direct connection to Harrods. After working there for so many years, they might well claim they own part of it. They visited Ixworth many times, and Tadzik would spend most of his time fishing in our local River Blackbourne. Sometimes he would bring up to an eighteen-inch pike, and there would be a celebration. Maryla was an expert in the preparation of the fish, either for the table or for the deep freeze. She would spend her time either in the sun in the garden or having a chat with my mother – that was what both of them enjoyed most. They would pull apart all our friends and families; it was a delightful sight to see those two ladies, one sipping her traditional cup of coffee, which would never be wasted, but only topped with a fresh supply.

Our life in Cheyne Walk was rich in every respect. Work, people, situation, schools and the general environment helped us to build our opinion gradually about this, our adopted country. So much so, in fact, that we already started to feel British.

The Zbirochowski-Koscia family, or rather Hania

Czarnocka, as was her maiden name, came quite early into our life. Firstly, both Hania and her mother, Halina, were known to Jola's family whilst Jola was a guide. They came from Krzeniemiec in eastern Poland, which is unfortunately now under Russian occupation. It was geographically and historically a very famous place, being known for its Lyceum, and grand houses. Not far away was Lawra Poczajowska, with its well-known Orthodox Russian church and monastery. Scores of people would come to visit it, and admire the very small triptych of the Madonna and Child, renowned for its healing qualities. Both Hania and her mother came via Italy to England, and our friendship, mostly through Jola, was renewed. After marrying Kazio, Hania managed to have six children, who were all very well brought up. Jola had the privilege to be godmother to the youngest daughter, Halusia.

The children speak magnificently in Polish and travel often to Poland, being proficient in Polish and English. Basia, the third child, managed to travel even to China, to teach English in a Chinese university. We always kept and still keep in contact with them.

Incidentally, Kazio, who worked for many years with the famous contracting firm Taylor Woodrow, became their leading designer, especially for bridges and pressure vessels for electricity-generating factories. He is a very able man and a very good father, having well embedded in him Roman Catholic principles.

Hania's mother, Mrs Czarnocka, is an extremely celebrated person in Polish circles and has, for many years, been in charge of the Polish History Institute and Museum. She is so devoted to her work (she is in her eighties now) that any money given to her for her imprisonment during the war by the Germans, she donates to maintain the Museum and Institute. I must take my hat off to this family, so too in fact to Danusia Sujkowska, who is her cousin, and who lived for some years in Battersea, where we used to meet, even living in Ramsden Road, and afterwards Cheyne Walk.

After Danusia's marriage to Danek Francki, we made a pact that we would all emigrate to Canada together. Both our families got our passports, visas and even the at that time nominal tickets (£10 only), but at that point the Canadian government temporarily stopped immigration. The result was that, for practical reasons, I got another job and we gave up thoughts of emigrating. On the other hand, they decided to go and they are living there even now, their lives full of both happy and unhappy events which struck their family life.

We met both Danusia and Danek some thirty years later, when they visited Europe for the first time since their departure. It was a very happy and memorable reunion. We felt like it was yesterday since we had said goodbye. I really have deep and hearty feelings towards this family.

Incidentally, before they married, Danusia lived in Battersea, with her brother and the Pilsudskis' family, a mother and two daughters, one of whom was an architect working for the GLC and the other was a glider pilot.

For those who are ignorant as to whom General Pilsudski was, he was the first leader of the freed Poland after one hundred years of occupation, which finished in 1919 – a celebrated and worshipped man for many people. He was actually nominated as 'Marshall'.

I have to apologise for making many diversions in my story, but it is very fortunate that so many isolated happenings, incidents or even whole stories helped to build me as I am today, and that is the purpose of this work.

From 15 May 1950 to 31 October 1951, I worked with the Twisteel Reinforcement Company in Upper Brook Street. I had already reached the stage of being a responsible designer in reinforced concrete work. What I was missing was the fact that all my nice designs, which were, many times, the envy of my colleagues, were not in fact seen by myself (at least not the end product). They included, a reinforced concrete chimney to the West Ham College, the creamery to the Glasgow factory which consisted of twelve entirely different barrel vaults of roof construction, and eventually the design of a stocking factory in Margate. That was under the supervision of Dr Hajnal-Koni. The drawings of this factory were published in the *Reinforced Concrete Journal*, and they were virtually at the close of my time with Twisteel Reinforcement Ltd.

I have missed many earlier incidents, facts and associated names. I decided to take leave of our life in 128 Cheyne Walk, on a ground floor in Milton Chambers. I proudly announced that the same firm of estate agents, London and Westcliff Property Co., offered us a flat on three levels, maisonette-type detached house. This was 9 Mayow Road, between Forest Hill and Sydenham. There was a large garden, with a beautiful pear tree at the rear, some one hundred-foot high. The amount of pears we used to collect annually could be easily counted in hundredweights. We gave them to as many friends as we could think of at the time.

The work on the house and on the garden was tremendous (if I recollect now how many times Jola and I had to repeat this work, the figure of four is the least number). But we enjoyed ourselves, because we were building our life, however difficult it would eventually prove to be.

I wanted to design and then to build what I had designed, and as a result on 28 September 1951, I was interviewed by EMK (Hayward), Deputy Chief Engineer of Trollope and Colls at 44 Great Victoria Street. I was accepted, with an annual salary of £650, and I began designing buildings I would never have imagined that I could be given full and very wide responsibilities during my twenty-three years of engineering with this firm. I have been responsible for numerous designs and supervision of some very important, almost monumental buildings. At one time, I was responsible for a staff of up to thirty engineers, some of them with very good degrees. They were happy to work with me because they were also interested in such significant projects, so much so that one year when there was a rail and bus strike, all of us would walk to the office from wherever we lived. Some would arrive only in time to go home, but the principle was established, and everyone was happy.

Although my firm moved many times whilst working with them, it was always the same and gave me a feeling of stability and prosperity for the future. That I needed very badly.

At that time, we were not thinking of another move; we were simply trying to organise our lives. We were under the impression that 9 Mayow Road was the turning point in our life. We were able to stop wandering, look back and take stock of our achievements, before we made our next move.

It was in Mayow Road that our five years of life in

Britain were completed, and we decided to change our nationality and to ask the Home Office to accept us for British citizenship. I said to change our nationality, because it was necessary to do it that way; according to the Polish Constitution, Poles could only have one nationality, unlike in Britain.

Firstly, therefore, we had to ask the Polish President (in exile in London) to be released from our Polish citizenship, if only to be polite. The reply came via the Polish Embassy in Dublin – there were two such official embassies outside the Polish regime in communist Poland: Dublin and the Vatican.

I received confirmation of my promotion in the army to the officers' rank. We simultaneously filled out the application form for British naturalisation. Because of the cost, only I asked for that privilege in the circumstances. Jola and Ingrid would automatically become British citizens, because their husband and father would be a naturalised subject. We were very carefully screened by the Home Office – an officer spent one whole day at our home in Mayow Road. However, on 22 February 1954, we received a certificate which had had to be sworn with the Commissioner for Oaths.

Before I finish with the story of my time at Trollope and Colls, I must say a few words about the man who originally employed me, and whose departure from our firm I witnessed.

Mr E M Hayward was one of our engineers, who never raised his voice, and who spent a colossal amount of time in furthering his knowledge of his subject. He knew his men very well, and could in many cases anticipate their reactions. He failed in this respect with me – I remember one instance, when I was awarded a very large increase in my salary, directly because of his influence. Nevertheless, he called me to his office and said, 'K,' (that's how I was titled) 'as from next month your salary will be increased by … money.'

I simply said, 'Thank you very much,' and, 'is that all?' and I turned round and proceeded to walk from his office.

'Just a moment, K, did you understand what I told you?' he asked.

'Yes,' I replied. 'I am very obliged for your recognition of my work.' And again I walked away.

Mr Hayward was simply astounded. Probably my life experience, my training in the Underground Army, my time in the concentration camps, taught me to behave like that. Or perhaps it was in my mind that I was never rewarded in proportion to my knowledge of and my devotion towards my work for the company, and this, therefore, produced such a reaction.

I owed a great deal to EMH, as he was called. One thing in particular, was his trust in my honesty and loyalty. That is why I would be given so much responsibility and was often not even checked. For those points I have a great, thank you, dear Manek.

Lastly, there was one incident that I will always remember. Someone was designing a twenty-storey hotel in Gibraltar, and made a mess of it. EMH took it from him, and passed it to me, without going into the background history. It was very noble of him to spare the dignity of that other designer. He knew that both I and many others would draw their own conclusions, but it was not spelled out by him.

I redesigned the building, and we had a nice few days in Gibraltar – I enjoyed it, even if eventually we did not get the job!

Trollope and Colls changed their headquarters four times during my employment with them. Every time we built our own office block. Each time it was better, larger and with a superior finish. Not because it was to be our headquarters, but because by selling it, the better value it would have.

There were many subjects connected directly with London that interested me greatly. Some are not known to ordinary citizens, as most of them are below the street levels. Here are some of them:

1) There are several services provided at different depths below the city of London and West End. Everyone knows about the Underground railway, but I do not know who realises that some of the tunnels were dug out in a very ingenious method by almost horizontally boring the huge tunnels. Unfortunately, there were mishaps.

For example, the Central Line tunnel between St Paul's and Chancery Lane Stations were drilled for each line from opposite ends.

It was unfortunate that the line from St Paul's was drilled slightly upwards, landing very high up. On the other hand, the second tunnel from Chancery Lane to St Paul's was slightly inclined downwards. The result was, that the escalators at both stations were of a different and opposing length. When you will think for a moment, this will become obvious.

2) Still about the Underground or as it is often called, the Tube. I have already described the Lotts Power Station, which provided electricity. The other important factor was ventilation. There were huge, almost vertical shafts, which provided free air circulation, achieved with the aid of large fans. I had the pleasure (at least it was interesting) to climb one such shaft at the Green Park

station, wearing a special outfit. It was necessary because of the pending construction of the Victoria Line. Dover House was a large building housing the upper part of that station. This six- or seven-storey building was built on very deep concrete blocks, which saddled over each tunnel of the Central Line. The Victoria Line was deeper, and in order to avoid any complications, which could endanger Dover House, its station was moved some few hundred yards further. However, the entrance at ground level was planned at the same Green Park station. (That is why there is such a long walk when you change from the Central Line to the Victoria Line.) Everything ended very satisfactorily, except for one thing. There exists under London another network of high pressure, large water pipes.

They are required as hydrants, which served the fire brigade hoses in case of fire, especially in very high buildings. One of these pipes was damaged during the construction work, unknown to anyone, and water (high pressurised) was pouring into the sub-basement of Dover House. Should that not have been discovered in time, who knows what the consequences could have been? The mind boggles! However, I was in such a situation many times.

3) There was another network of tunnels under central London. There was the Post Office miniature railway, at much greater depth, linking certain sorting offices. When I was designing piling construction to Newgate house, I was asked by the local authority to submit my piling layout to the Ministry of Post and Telegraph. This was duly returned with approval, but with no explanations. I had been working long enough in London to realise that my building was close to such a

railway. Nevertheless, it was considered as a close secret, and we respected it as such.

4) The other underground tunnelling was, and still is, for Smithfield Market storages. The huge lorries, loaded with meat carcasses, would drive underground to leave their cargo in the deep-freeze storage. I don't know how many tons of meat is stored there, but I think it could be compared with the EEC mountains of butter or milk. After a fire at one of the overground halls, which spread underground, the fat and meat were burning for many days. It was an experience I will remember always.

5 Beaver House was a centre for storing animal skins, thousands and thousands of them, from ordinary sheepskins to the most expensive ermine, silver fox or minks. Many well-off people would store their fur coats there during the summer months. The storage was within a double basement, which was fully refrigerated. My visit to this place was to ascertain the possible effect on the adjoining Underground station, and several important buildings, should the refrigeration be stopped for whatever reason. About ten to twenty foot around and below was frozen solid, and any thawing would certainly cause some soil movements. It was one of those experiences that you only have once in your life, and where your decision is very important indeed. This was a category of job that did not provide my firm with a lot of income. Probably it more often ran at a loss; but it was required for the prestige of Trollope and Colls, or as it was later, Trafalgar House. I was proud to participate on numerous occasions.

My company had a reputation for traditional quality of workmanship, not just making a profit; this was our motto. Should that not have been the case, then it would not have managed for more than a decade since I joined the firm, to be more or less the only construction company in the city of London. It was almost unthinkable for anyone else to secure a contract with the banks, insurance companies, livery halls, churches, and government buildings. The reputation of Trollope and Colls was beyond reproach.

I remember the words of Mr Potter, our very good engineer/director, who gave me a pep talk, his words always rang in my ears: 'My boy, when you go to the site, your main interest must be the standard of work – not the quickness; that aspect you have to leave to the manager. Should you see anything that in your eyes, as an engineer, is not only dangerous, but below the best standard, you must insist that the foreman or manager should put things right; if this does not succeed, then you must go to the directors. It is our reputation that is at stake.'

He was so right, and believe me, I passed that opinion every time I visited a site, small or large. Our foremen had such a good reputation that much too often an insurance company, bank, or newspaper firm would pinch them to be their own clerk-of-works on a good salary.

I must mention newspapers. I think with the exception of the *Daily Mirror* that we built the offices of every one of them. One could then say that Fleet Street belonged to Trollope and Colls. There were of course good architects, good engineering firms and very good quantity surveyors. However, even they relied on our reputation. It meant that whatever they designed, we would construct and finish in the best possible way. We had the best tradesmen, like the

Leach family of bricklayers; they learnt their jobs from their fathers and grandfathers. Our firm was the best promoter of good quality apprenticeships. I remember that for a good tradesman, the minimum apprenticeship would be not less than seven years. People were, like myself, always proud of the results.

The other point which I think is extremely important, was that I would never be paid extra if a setting out job had to be done on a Sunday. I might be given a day off in lieu, but no extra payment. There was once an extremely interesting situation. My chief engineer/director was on holiday, and I was in charge. One of the newspaper firms asked me whether I could get three or four engineers to do some extra work on levelling their long presses (over one hundred-foot long) during Saturday and Sunday. They told me they would give each man an extra £50 for this work. At first, it appeared to me to be quite in order, and I organised such a team. They did the job to everyone's satisfaction. That was, with the exception of our managing director, who was told in passing how good his engineers were. You should have heard what a telling off I received for that incident. I was told that in no circumstances could such an incident be repeated. The firm repaid the £150 – with apologies, and assurances that its staff would carry out any work, whether in office hours or outside hours, free of charge.

I was told: 'You are employed, like doctors, nurses or firemen, to work whenever you are required. The only assumption is that your working week is forty-five hours [as it was then], and you may claim free time if you have worked more than those hours.' It reminded me very well of my first practice in Poland. The principle was always that, 'the job has to be done first – then you can rest.' I wish people would have that principle today.

There were times when I would be telephoned on Saturday evening to come to the city of London. The telephone call would be either from my directors, managers of various jobs, the District Surveyor, or the Dangerous Structure Inspector (such a post only existed in the city of London).

One incident of such a nature I remember was when the Grocer's Hall was almost completely burnt out. It was a magnificent structure, but mostly timber. It was very close to the Bank of England building. I arrived as soon as I could, with Mr Barker, the Safety Officer; we walked through this enormous building, or rather, its remains. At one point, Mr Barker turned to me and said, 'Look Mr Kasicki, you are covered in blood.' It was true. I had walked bareheaded (my fault), and when passing under a burnt-out oak beam, I touched with my head the razor sharp remains of a beam. I had not noticed it. A wipe of my handkerchief solved the problem. It was decided after inspection that the building was to be pulled down, as it was beyond repair.

I will not bother you with stories of the dozens of other buildings in the city constructed, checked or rebuilt at this period of time, but a few words about the Grocer's Hall, I am sure, will not go amiss.

It was a three-storey building. The ground floor was mostly offices. An enormous timber staircase led to the first floor, which was a magnificent structure. The main hall, where the functions were held, consisted of a very beautiful floor of about 200 foot by 100 foot, an uninterrupted area.

There were three fantastic chandeliers with hundreds of crystal pendants and beautiful crystal candle holders converted into electricity. The chandeliers weight was about half ton each. All had dropped to the ground during that raging fire. They were suspended from a very big, long, wrought iron steel beam, which in addition to holding these chandeliers also supported the floor construction above. These beams were constructed, as they say, in situ. In other words, in place, because they would be too long and too heavy, if manufactured elsewhere, both for transportation and for placing. How then, were all rivets placed and hammered in? The headroom was about twenty foot or more. The beam was assembled on scaffolding at the right level. It was composed of many thick, wide, wrought iron plates. The blacksmith-type fire was burning on the floor below. The white-hot rivets were picked by expert men who threw them up to other men standing on a platform above, who were wearing thick leather gloves with special padding across the palms of the hands. These men immediately placed the rivets into the pre-drilled holes. With the help of other men with special hammers, standing on the reverse side of this beam, the whole beam was assembled. It was a slow but very exact process, when hundreds of such rivets would be fixed. A really magnificent achievement. I looked and looked at those beams. They were still in their position after the fire.

The kitchens were on the floor above. There was another thing which caught my eye. There was a huge fireplace, with large flues. The central one was about fifteen to twenty-foot wide. On either side there were two smaller ones, for the purpose of producing enough draught in order that the chain-driven spit arrangement could be put into action. The main spit could accommodate two oxen at one time, or sixty chickens, to be roasted simultaneously. At the floor level, there was a nearly twenty-foot long by four-foot wide steel trough, where the dripping fat could be collected.

The hall was big enough to entertain and feed up to 300 people at one time. The kitchens were on the top floor in order that the fumes and smell would be kept away from the guests.

I could write pages about this one building, but there is neither a place for it in my book, nor would the reader be interested in such structural matters. One thing could conclude this particular story; that after enquiring with the fire service, and the insurance people, I found the reason for this fire. It was very simple. The nightwatchman had forgotten to switch off the electric light under the main stairs, which was located between the supporting beams. A slight draught over the overheated beams created a spark, causing a fire to start on the tinder-dry timber stairs.

One of the other outstanding stories connected with governmental and royal buildings in the Westminster area was the admiralty bunker near Old Scotland Yard, one of my first jobs with Trollope and Colls. I was, therefore, already familiar with some people who were in charge of such buildings. One person who was responsible on behalf of the Ministry of Works with that kind of job was Mr Fox.

I had the pleasure of being connected with three separate jobs in the Houses of Parliament. First were the lifts in the House of Lords. Second, there was the press building, which was directly linked to the House of Commons and the House of Lords. Thirdly, there was quite involved work on the crypt, under the Houses of Parliament. One more job has also come to my mind, which was the strengthening of Big Ben's tower.

I had to be in frequent contact with Mr Fox, and I remember when telephoning his office, the reply was, 'Oh, he is not here at the moment, but he may be either in Buckingham Palace, or St James's Palace, or in the Whitehall Buildings.' I was never in Buckingham Palace, but I helped in the construction of the extension to the National Gallery, which adjoins its grounds.

I would like to make one or two more comments on my work with Trollope and Coll. I remember our pipe yard in Camberley, where I spent many days testing concrete pipes of special design to destruction done totally by me. Our director, Mr Browning, together with myself and the directors of the Stanton and Redlands firms, used to meet for a working luncheon in the Cafe Royale, Tudor Suite, to discuss progress on our findings, which might be incorporated in the new code of practice for the pipes design. I was very impressed by flying to Cumbria, twice I think, again to our yard where pipes were produced, but at that time, clad and reinforced with nylon thread dipped in special resins. Incidentally, the last time I visited Camberley, I was amazed at the hundreds of pre-cast units for the new Stock Exchange, also by a new method of constructing concrete pipes by a spinning method.

The other yard that needs mentioning was Camberwell, where the timbering and plastering departments were located. The fibrous plasterwork produced by their chief, Vallone, was beyond any price. I do not imagine anyone else could or would have been able to lower the Adam ceiling in the club in King Edward Street. It was necessary to lower the ceiling to accommodate a new floor construction, as the original one was already rotting away.

The Adam ceiling was in three colours, and was one of the most beautiful made. We cut it into small sections of squares of two foot or so, and we constructed a very tight platform covered with thick felt. This was supported by a forest of props, especially decorated in order that the distinguished members could use their club and not be disturbed. I saw some of them fully asleep in the club chairs, completely unaware of what was happening above their heads.

The Carlton Houses in the Mall were another example of good, solid craftsmanship. During the war, all these houses had accommodated mostly the Foreign Office, and the Ministry of the Interior. Before the war, they accommodated all embassies, including Hitler's embassy in England. It is worth mentioning that all these buildings, which were built about 250 years ago, were in the style used by Italian craftsmen. The German Embassy had taken great efforts to cover the original, beautiful Italian artistry with Germanic-type geometrical false constructions. There were now garages where in Victorian times there were kitchens, where the whole pig would once been slaughtered and transferred on a pulley system to the butcher's table.

I have to mention one of the foremen, Mr Noaks, an outstanding man in many ways. In my time, we together rebuilt the whole of Gray's Inn Law Society, including the chapel. The hall was rebuilt before my time, under the supervision and design of my best friend Earnshaw-Wall. He was a very old-fashioned engineer, but in the early stages, he was my main guide, I could even say, my guru. I still keep in contact with his wife, Rose. He held the respect of everyone, especially his right-hand man Mr William Paine. I could write pages about Gray's Inn, but there was also Lincoln's Inn Law Society. I must also add a few words about Fenchurch Street. It was the first building of its kind, twenty-two or twenty-three floors with a raft of fifteen foot, tapering along the perimeter to about eight foot.

It was constructed on many drilled and concreted in situ piles, about four foot six inches in diameter, but under-rimmed at eighty foot down to a very impressive fourteen-foot diameter. They formed what we call an inverted mushroom. I went down to one or two of these piles. You have to concrete them not more than four hours after drilling, to avoid collapse.

For me it was a great experience. Wearing a helmet – that was the only protection I had – and armed with powerful torches, I went with the foreman to the bottom of that impressive shaft. Shielding ourselves as best we could from falling debris, we were lowered in an open steel bucket. I was thinking that in this way, one could build a very effective atomic shelter.

The core of the building, containing staircases, lifts and sanitary equipment, who constructed with sliding shuttering. When the core was constructed, I had again the unusual experience of climbing the 300-foot core with the help of ladders placed floor by floor. There was a magnificent view of the whole of London. Nevertheless, we were waiting for structural steel, which would project around the top of the core, forming a twenty-five-foot platform along the whole perimeter. From the ends of that platform, there would be flat steel hangers that would support future floors, one by one.

To do this, one would have to construct an unobtrusive means to get access to the top. This was my job, and I was proud that I could design and construct a tubular structure that would contain two goods lifts and access platforms at two levels.

I required about 500 steel tubes and ten-foot thick concrete, forming the anchoring block below. I must quickly say that no one ever checked my design; but it worked excellently.

When this temporary tower was constructed, it was a lovely ride, much preferred to climbing the ladders, to reach the top. Incidentally, the steel for the roof construction was to be provided and welded, with the high tensile 'I' sections of beams, with flanges four inches thick. The manufacturers, Dorman Long, had failed twice to produce them. Eventually, with the team of engineers from Ove Arup Partners, pre-stressed concrete construction was designed and supported on the temporarily erected Bailey Bridge platform. It was a tremendous feat of engineering, and that building dominated the Fenchurch Street area.

Meeting this team of engineers from the Ove Arup Partners was an experience all on its own. My boss, E M Hayward, went with me to their offices, where we met a senior partner and a team of five engineers, each an expert in his own field. There was a senior designer, a planning expert, a coordinator with different manufacturers. Within an hour or so, the whole problem was fully discussed, explained, and put to work. I admired their organisation, and this top class efficiency and expertise.

There was of course the Holborn development, which was totally after my design. It contained a new road, with the garages underneath, and two rows of houses on either side of the road, with varying heights, up to six storeys high. It was parallel to the Holborn Street frontage, and spanning high enough to let London buses pass under (fourteen foot six inches). The span of the bridge was some seventy-three foot, and the bridge was supported on four reinforced concrete columns, two foot each in diameter, each accommodating twelve, two-inch-diameter steel bars. It was a very interesting job, especially as the bars had to be placed by crane, because of their weight.

As there was no British Code of Practice to design reinforced concrete bridges, which would be continuous over many supports and carrying a new road, I made my own design and went to the Ministry of Transport to meet the people who originated the Code of Practice. After a few hours of discussion, my method was accepted and my design approved. There were many similar situations, but there is neither the space nor the need for such explanations.

Among so many other jobs, two outstanding constructions of Berkeley Hotel and offices, also Broad Street House, both of which were almost finished when I had to depart from Trollope and Colls, and Trafalgar House, in 1972.

After having a lovely send-off from both Trollope and Colls, and Trafalgar House, I felt on the one hand, very sorry to be leaving so many great memories of friendship, comradeship and appreciation, but I also realised how much effort I had put into my twenty-three years there. Besides the jobs I have already mentioned, I have to add that my place of employment was changed at least five times. I experienced so many things, which are deeply engraved in my body and heart.

I will always remember the people in charge, like Mr McNamara, Mr West, Mr Mais, who eventually became Lord Mais and then Lord Mayor of London, as well as the triumphant return of Victor Matthews with Nigel Broackes. Victor is now Lord Matthews, Managing Director of Trafalgar House Company.

Among my past directors, there was D W (Wark) Potter, whom I greatly admired, and so many others. Special mention is due to both Colin Mansfield and Alan Ure, especially Colin, who told me that, when he was a junior engineer, his career was predicted by computer. This method was then in the experimental stage but popular with the wealthy. In Colin's case the computer predicted that engineering was most suitable for him, when in fact he was always interested in people and social problems. It was obvious when he worked on a new community in Wales he was very good and he enjoyed his work. I precisely remember when he was sent to Trawsfynydd Power Station in Wales, which our firm built, to organise the village for about 4,000 workers and their families. He did the job extremely well, was one of the best organisers, socially minded, and of course he enjoyed himself doing that kind of job – that was Colin! He is now a very competent Managing Director of Construction and Development in Trollope and Coll, together with Alan Ure.

I remember Alan Ure (brother of the famous actress) on my first job, on the admiralty bunker, next to Old Scotland Yard. I was very impressed with his performance, especially when he had to deal with tons of water pouring all round. The excavations were nearly 200 foot below ground level. Fifteen foot-thick basement slabs and retaining walls, secured the future of that work. It was very funny when on the completion of the structure, no one knew whether the bunker had sunk or risen, as the reference level was taken on the steps of Old

Scotland Yard adjoining the structure. I think it was finally decided that the Scotland Yard had moved upwards.

When we were taken over by Trafalgar House, new offices were provided again, this time for a larger unit. The building was on the corner of King Street and Berkeley Square.

It was very funny to realise that just before the take-over. I was directed once to see the agent of that particular building by the Distillers' Co., who owned a very prestigious building with centuries of tradition, but which was adjoining the future Trafalgar House offices. I met Mr Reeves, who was the agent for Bridge-Walkers, the builders. I agreed with him and with the Distillers' Surveyor the method of protection for the Distillers' Co. building. Mr Reeves is now, or was until recently, managing director of Trollope and Colls. What a coincidence!

However, the inevitable happened. Trafalgar House succeeded in taking Trollope and Colls under their umbrella. We were followed by Cementation, by Cunard including the QE2, by the *Daily Express*, and by a host of other enterprises small and larger.

Even now, there is talk about erecting a large bridge over the Thames to connect two ends of the M25, in East London.

On the whole, we have done quite well. Even my unfrozen pension is now better than if it would have been under Trollope and Colls.

We moved to the King's Street building and after-wards to Mitcham, where approximately 4,000 staff for the whole £225 million organisation worked. However, it was in the minds of both Nigel Broackes, the Chairman, and Victor Matthews, the managing director, that a prestigious building must be built for Trafalgar House in the West End of London.

The site of the old Berkeley Hotel, was purchased, and the architects, Chapman, Taylor and Partners, but particularly Jane Durham and Edward Best, were chosen to do the design. It was a pleasure to work with them, and with our managers like Carter and Urving, and with the quantity surveyors, Gardiner and Teobald, and with David Male. I know it took years, but the results were the best I have seen for many, many years. I left the firm soon after the 'topping' ceremony. I was given many letters of sorrow, but also of congratulations, and I am proud to have been the designer of the Berkeley Complex. We even managed to design and build the internal staircase, between the first and second floors (between Nigel Broackes' and Victor Matthews' offices), which looked out of this world. For me it was the 'Eighth' Wonder of the World.

The Broad Street House, near Liverpool Street Station was an impressive building; there was no comparison to the intricacy of the Berkeley Complex. I think the £8 million was well spent; a memorial to Trafalgar House. There is one little postscript. On the opposite side of Piccadilly there is the Savoy Restaurant, the best in London, which Nigel and Victor frequented very often. But now they would overlook it from their windows. It was not possible – they bought it!

I cannot get away from life and work, with both Trollope and Colls and Trafalgar House. As I said earlier, my, as I called him, guru, Mr Earnshaw-Wall, really introduced me not only to Trollope and Colls, but to the city of London. He was an absolute mine of knowledge, a very practical man, not only as a good engineer, but like myself he was interested and involved in many other facets of life, including photography, radio, recording, field engineering and history.

When I said that I was engaged in either rebuilding, building from new, or contributing to the conservation of many buildings, in the city of London, this included many livery companies and their precious halls. Mr Earnshaw-Wall had been doing this since the very end of the war, or even probably during the war.

When he retired I compiled an album of photographs that I had taken of the city buildings he was personally connected with in his professional capacity. It was, I can assure you, a very substantial album. His wife Rose, with whom I still correspond, was his very beloved companion.

There was a little incident when I was working still in Great Queen Street. I was very interested, besides photography and radio, in watches. I would go during my lunch hour to the Leather Lane market, beside the original shop of Gamages. It was only a one-hour market, and I have described it in another part of my story. I bought there a very small Rolex watch, which did not work. After careful examination, I found that besides being dirty, the main spring was broken. Clerkenwell was a street where all parts for watches could be bought. I got a new spring, which was not more than half a centimetre in diameter. I was so excited that I decided to fix it into the watch in the remaining minutes of my lunch hour. It was a disaster. The spring and its casing flicked into the air, and landed somewhere in the office.

The whole staff, including Mr Earnshaw-Wall, were searching for over an hour. Finally, it was found and fitted, to everyone's admiration and satisfaction. It was not the only time that office hours were interrupted.

The watch was fully serviced by Rolex and my daughter wore it proudly as a present from her father.

I was looking another day in a little booklet of Trollope and Colls, listing the directors, and their projects before and after the war. I then ticked those projects which I had been personally involved in. But I do not like to boast, and I will not give you that figure.

However, one job which I think will always stand out in my mind was the courtroom of Tallow-Chandlers Hall. It was the first courtroom built in London, and it was the only one left. Unfortunately, the oak beam construction (dating from 1462) started to deteriorate. It was my privilege to carry out such reconstruction, keeping as near as possible to the original, but retaining its structural stability.

It was painstakingly done, and when completed, for a joke I sat in the judge's seat, condemning all my craftsmen to death by hanging. It was a very proud moment. This building was very close to Cannon Street Station.

There were scores of other contracts. Trollope and Colls, used to have a branch in Portsmouth called JNO Croad Ltd. I was therefore a frequent visitor to Portsmouth. One of the biggest contracts there was Landport Drapery Bazaar; it was a really big job, and I was very proud of it. We used to have a big board that said, 'Watch how it grows'. It certainly grew! There was Lloyds Bank, and a very interesting job in Gosport (you have to cross on the ferry to get there). It was Gosport Ritz Cinema. It was the first time I designed a reinforced brick beam, spanning more than seventy foot over the balcony. I was very proud of it, and I hope it is still there.

Talking about Lloyds Bank, I think I have constructed, designed or reconstructed, three of their banks, in the city of London, one in Portsmouth and one in Birmingham. The last one was extremely interesting, on two points:

1) The design was by one eminent consulting engineer – which we found to be wrong.

2) There was one tenant on the site, who would not vacate his home during the demolition stage of the old buildings. We decided to incorporate him in the new Lloyds offices. I hope he is still there.

I did say earlier that I do not want to boast, and what am I doing? I am praising my achievements all the time. Please excuse such indulgence. But there were so many things which happened during my twenty-three years with this one firm, which had well over 200 years of experience, that I feel I have a full right to my elation.

I do not know whether one can feel as I do, that I got to know the city of London so well that I felt it would be a part of me I will never forget. When my mother came from Poland, I drove her around the city, as we used to call it, to show her my jobs. She would hardly believe it when the foremen came out to greet me and her on many occasions. For her it was like a dream.

One of my jobs was to carry out the strengthening of Tower Bridge, as one of its towers was cracking badly. The job was done, and I took my mother to look into the machinery operating the bridge. The engineer knew me, and was very happy to show it to my mother. It was another milestone.

Another very interesting contract was for the St Paul's

Choir School, which was being built behind St Paul's Cathedral. I used to walk for years on the other side of Queen Street, where the boys were temporarily accommodated. I always stopped and listened to their singing.

The new site was on the fully demolished area behind St Paul's, where a small St Augustine's church used to be. Of that church, only the remains of the tower were saved. Nevertheless, the new steeple was constructed out of fibreglass, and lowered into position by helicopter. This was to be part of the new Choir School, and I was very proud to be responsible for its construction, in the best of craftsmen's style.

There is one little postscript to that. The area behind St Paul's was, in the past, used for all sorts of religious processions. Therefore, the streets were named according to the responses which would be sung, such as Ave Maria Lane, Pater Noster. That area was also the place where in 1665, during the Plague of London, most of the bodies were buried in a common grave. When we had to carry out the excavations, scores of human bones were found. It was therefore decided that the dean of St Paul's would deconsecrate the excavation, and any remains would be properly buried. It was an almost impossible task, and our men were digging on a 'bonus' basis. It was therefore, a rather tragicomic situation, when the different lorries would be loaded with bones if the dean was looking the other way.

These old burial areas were always a very great problem in the city. There are still plaques for the known burial areas, but who knows about others?

I have not said anything about Trinity House, in Tower Hill. Trinity House was almost totally destroyed by the blitz. It, along with all its masters (Prince Consort,

Albert and Winston Churchill were acting members), controls all the movements of shipping along the Thames and around Britain; it controls all the lighthouses and tugs.

I was responsible for rebuilding the whole area, which included a new office block and the reconstruction of both the Wyatt building and the banqueting hall, in the design of the architect, Professor Richardson. It was a very impressive building, with a great history. I remember being shown the passage between the anteroom, and the courtroom, where, in the extremely wide wall, there was a little flap where a potty would be placed for the weakness in Prince Albert's condition. There were (and are) two sets of large doors, and between them would be that tiny loo. A fascinating story.

As you may well know, there are two places in London, where you can express your personal opinions on any subject, so long as you are standing on a soapbox. One is Hyde Park Corner, and the other is Trinity Square, next to the Tower of London. I mention this, because I had a young woman engineer, who belonged to the Free Church, and who would regularly go there to preach – I am afraid she had to leave our firm.

There is one more story attached to the area of the Tower of London and Tower Bridge. One of our friends, who had been a colonel in the Polish cavalry, died. It was his wish that his body should be returned to Poland. His wife, Mela, made all the arrangements.

The coffin was fixed on the deck of the Polish ship, and the widow was told that on a given night, at 2 a.m., the ship would be passing under Tower Bridge. We lived then in Mayow Road, so she came to us and I promised to take her to see the ship passing under Tower Bridge.

We arrived about three-quarters of an hour early, and waited patiently for over an hour. Finally, I decided to go to the Tower Bridge control room (I was familiar there) and ask them where the Polish ship was. 'Oh,' they said, 'it left two hours ago.' I was very sorry for Mela.

Now is the time when the second stage of the education of my children could be described.

Ingrid, as I said earlier, had been for some time in La Sagesse Convent School in Golders Green. From there, in 1953, she automatically transferred to St Winifred's Convent School, almost opposite our home at 9 Mayow Road. I think Ingrid was very happy there.

Olgierd's education proceeded in a slightly different way. In 1951, he was still in Reigate with Miss Welch, until he reached his fifth year of age. He was mostly at home after returning from Reigate, where he was eventually very much more settled than at the beginning. When Jola and I went to see him in Miss Welch's home, he would not even speak to us; only after two hours of touring Reigate, would he once more be our son again. This period was very painful for us, but after all, we had to earn enough money for the rent, travel to work, decoration of the house and Ingrid's education. This was the only possible way for us, to keep him for a relatively short time with Miss Welch, who was extremely devoted to the Polish people.

Whilst living in Mayow Road, we sent Olgierd for a very short time to a nursery school, which was attached to Sydenham Catholic School. This was an extreme failure, and we had to remove him from there very soon indeed. At the required age of five years, he was sent to Christ Church School, run by the LCC in Forest Hill. He was there from 1954 to 1957. It was an Anglican school run by a very strict headmaster, Mr R A C Brough, BSc. As our family was Roman Catholic, we were told that Olgierd would be admitted on one condition – that we (I) would take him every Sunday to the Anglican Church in Forest Hill.

In those two years, we got to know the vicar of this church, and I found that, being a very high church, there was hardly any difference between this and our Catholic churches. We met the vicar not only on Sundays, but in our house several times. He was a very humane man; this made us very proud that Olgierd had attended this school.

On the other hand, in those years, passing the eleven-plus exam, was like opening the gates for the future of a boy. Unfortunately, Mr Brough's school did not hold that opinion and as they say, *nolens volens*, we had no choice but to transfer Olgierd to St Winifred's Convent School, already known to us. This had been well proven by Ingrid's educational results. Before I leave Mr Brough's school, I must add a very small incident, which I don't think could happen today.

We had to buy Olgierd full school uniform, which was very expensive, but he looked grand in it. Unfortunately, on the second day at school, our absent-minded son lost his brand new coat, over a distance that was probably half a mile.

Believe it or not, the coat was left hanging on some-one's front garden railings; there were still honest people about. At those times Olgierd showed casualness with his possessions. In 1958, Olgierd joined St Winifred's Convent School, where eventually, after three years, he passed his eleven-plus examination, to our great relief.

It was at that precise time, when the decision would have to be taken about his secondary education. In those days, one's hands were very much tied, and one had to adhere to what St Winifred's Convent School would advise. In Olgierd's case, the choice was either the Silesians in Clapham, or the Jesuits in another part of London. Unfortunately, our opinions differed very much, and I had to face an extremely embarrassing conversation with Mother Mary Anastasia, the headmistress of St Winifred's. I could not go into details, as it would be unfair to the lady. Suffice it to say that we decided to enter Olgierd for Dulwich College. He passed the entrance examination in 1959, but I will tell this story later. All I can tell you now is that we were not the best Roman Catholics in Mother Mary Anastasia's eyes!

Now to Jola. Even when working with Bateman Cleaners, she spared no time in learning English, on a part-time correspondence course. She got a first class certificate on 13 August 1948, in Regent Street Polytechnic. The following year, she passed the general intermediate examinations in Physics, for internal students, whilst studying at Woolwich Polytechnic. It was another nine years before she was eventually awarded a certificate of approval of candidature for BA in English, French and History (January 1965). One must, of course, remember that it was her great struggle to obtain that certificate from the University of London.

It was in 1964 that Jola obtained A Levels in English Literature and History, as well as Latin and Polish. In 1962, she started working as a member of the staff of Save the Children Fund, at their HQ, until 1964, when she decided to study full-time for her teaching degree.

A senior lecturer at the Kingston College of Technology said, 'Despite the extra difficulties she faced, Jola expected no special treatment as a student. I think on the whole she enjoyed, and certainly benefited, from her three years at this college, in obtaining a BA degree, which she fully deserves.' This was signed, 'P Alderman, MA, PhD, Senior Lecturer, Kingston College of Technology'.

It is very difficult to follow Jola's achievements in the general examinations for external students, when she was included in the 1967 pass list. It would not be out of place to note that during the German occupation, she passed the Underground Studies in Organic Chemistry, Physics and General Biology at university level. This document was issued by London University on 11 February 1948, and countersigned by the rector, Father Czubalski. Just before war broke out, Jola passed general matriculation in the following subjects: Religious Education, Polish, French, History, Geography, Biology, Physics, Astronomy, Chemistry, Mathematics, Elements of Philosophy, Drawing and Gymnastics.

Music was another aspect of our family life. We purchased an upright piano. Both Ingrid and Olgierd passed up to Grade IV when learning to play this instrument. However, both of them gave it up, and only now, having their own families, are they repeating this story of learning to play any sort of instrument, including the piano.

They now realise how difficult it is to persuade their children to do their daily exercises. It is a great pity when you think you could help your son or daughter to play the piano even up to the standard you were at in your teens.

Our move to Sunderland Road, was another milestone in our life. The house was a type of maisonette, where we were living on the top floor. I remember how the removal people had an almost impossible task to get our piano up the last flight of stairs. After unscrewing the main door, they managed to get it in, but it was touch-and-go for a while.

The man who lived below us was never at home, because he worked every night at the telephone exchange – what a life.

Incidentally, as usual, I have missed one extremely important incident. In Mayow Road, the first floor was occupied by a very rich, black man and a very young, very blonde, Austrian girl. There were colossal arguments in their flat, and our children were petrified. The police arrived at my request, but could do nothing, as they said it was a domestic affair; however, they waited on the opposite side of the street. I was simply so upset that I broke the glass of the front door with a hammer. This was the signal for the police to move in and remove the culprits, to our relief.

My mother came for her first month's holiday to Sunderland Road. The following year, after several warnings from us that life here would be far from paradise, she decided to ask for permanent transfer to England.

With our invitation, after a long struggle, my mother arrived; by that time we had moved to Underhill Road. So we had two mothers, two children, two cats and one dog. People thought, at the very least, that it was very unwise!

The whole family were great animal lovers. You probably remember that on day one of my life, I was given a fox terrier.

In London, the first dog was brought home by Jola, when she worked at Bateman Cleaners. They had a dog which, because it was 'in season', had to be kept in the small stone yard. The dog escaped, and after being recaptured, the owners decided to have her put to sleep. Jola took pity, and brought her home; she was our first dog in England, and was called Lena. She was a chow of quite good breeding; she was with us for many years and eventually died of cancer.

Our life was many times affected by that illness whether in human friends or in animals. Lena's successor was also a chow, called Meme – she also died of cancer after a long illness; as did our friendly mongrel Olive. I had to have Olive put down, when Jola was also dying of that horrible illness. We are now left with only our cat Jessica, a blue Burmese. We had four other cats, and all of them finished their lives rather tragically.

Very recently we acquired a little puppy called Hugo, he is a Cavalier King Charles, and is a great challenge to me.

The following two digressions take us back to the early years of our life in London. It is, however, because, I hate today's London as a city, that the sentiment of London is still with me, especially of the late forties and the beginning of the fifties. Those were the times when I, as a young engineer, plunged myself, my wife and my family into the deep end of the connected problems of life in that strange city.

The city was strange in many ways. For instance, there was the colossal wealth of the institutions, like banks, building societies, livery halls and, of course, churches. All were concentrated in that one square mile of the city of London. On the other hand, you had poor people living in the slums of the East End.

The tradesmen's streets, like Ironmongers' Street, Furniture Street, Cabinet-makers' Street, Watchmakers' Street, Fruiterers' Street and scores of others. I will never forget the Leather Lane market, where for one hour of lunch break, scores of stalls would be open. Charlie the paint king, the stall for the best shoes at half price, iron tools – this I really envied; Kaskie, as he was called. How it would profit him to bring carts of ironmongery, I do not know. There was also a man selling sweets, who would be very rude with his own versions of nursery rhymes, like 'Mary had a little lamb', or 'I am Jim, from Notting Hill, who never worked, and never will'.

I remember Hatton Garden, where a number of Orthodox Jews would parade, doing, I am sure, very good business. Of course, one must not forget Petticoat Lane. This was a unique place for Londoners. They even rebuilt the area, and provided for a new Petticoat Lane.

I always wondered why there were so many banks of the same name in almost every street. There were ceremonies like the Lord Mayor's Show every year; our one-time managing director, Mr Mais, was once elected as Lord Mayor. As the procession and banquet were to be provided by the new Lord Mayor, I daresay that Mr Mais must have had considerable help from Trollope and Colls. Nevertheless, it was a splendid time.

The Bells of Bow reminded one of the nursery rhyme; I have visited them several times, with great admiration. One thing, on looking back, which I could never understand, was how many times I was given a free hand to reconstruct a building, without anyone checking what I was doing. But I was proud that it always proved to be a success.

Other events, connected with the city of London, I have already briefly described earlier in my story.

Jola was greatly involved in organising her school friends before the war. When I got to know her, during the last few months before the beginning of the war, and in the four years up to the Warsaw Uprising, I was very much adopted by her circle of friends. A few of them went through the uprising, and then their pack was divided into those who stayed behind in Poland as civilians, and the other group who went into the POW camps, like Maryla, Jola and many others. As a consequence, nearly all of those who left Poland, found themselves in Maczkow (Harren), in north-west Germany, where they were placed by the Polish First Armoured Division, under General Maczek. Many of them moved also to the Second Polish Corps in Italy under General Anders, the Polish leader. Maczkow, as I described earlier, was where Jola and I married.

What I have not explained was how, after the war, when contact with those in Poland was restored, it was firstly by a very erratic postal service, but later people could travel from East to West, and vice versa. Polish citizens could, on the grounds of a written invitation, visit their relatives and friends. At the very beginning, by the communist rule, they had to leave behind their close relatives as guarantors of their return. These rules were later relaxed and some, like Jola's mother, and later my mother, were permitted to leave Poland for good. My mother-in-law was one of the first people to get such a permit.

During our more than forty-year stay in England, both we and our friends managed to visit our relatives and friends. Poland badly needed foreign currency, like American dollars, and British pounds, and that was the reason for the relaxation. We had several visits from my cousin, and from Jola's friends, Zosia Zawadzka, and Iza Holderna, who lived in Warsaw. Sadly, Zosia died a few years ago.

Zosia and Iza came to London several times, and I cherish the memory of those visits very much. Zosia and Jola had hours of talk together. When Jola and I went to Poland in 1976, she met all the girls from her guide pack. The other two times I visited Poland, I was very well received. Once I went with my present wife, Maxine, who was very happy to see Warsaw and Kielce, and my grammar school. We had many parties at the homes of Jola's friends. We stayed in Zosia's and Iza's flat for the whole week in 1984.

We are still in contact with our friends in Warsaw, and with our Polish friends in London and Wolverhampton. Also we have friends who emigrated to Australia, Sweden and Canada. We have kept contact with Jola's family friends in the USA. They are Genio and Irene, who are now in happy retirement; luckily they left Poland, only days before the war started.

On leaving the Save the Children Fund, Jola was given a tremendous send-off; she was leaving to finish her degree course. She was then forty-two years old, having the household, including her mother, myself and two children, to look after.

It would certainly not be out of place to mention that during our stay at Mayow Road, Jola worked on the translation of books by a famous Polish writer called Jan Dobraczynski. It was then that he visited us in London, and gave her written authorisation to translate fragments of his novel, *Drzewa Chodzace*, ('Walking Trees'), for the *Anthology of the Modern Polish Mind*.

This brings me to a rather important fact, which affected our life in Mayow Road. We had made two new acquaintances, Mr and Mrs Kuncewicz, who lived almost across the road from us, past the convent school. Mrs

Kuncewicz was a very celebrated writer who, even before the war, started a series on Polish radio, which was very similar to *Mrs Dale's Diary* in England. Her series was extremely popular in Poland. She wrote scores of books, which were translated into many languages, like German, Swedish, Norwegian, American, and Canadian, leaving her with many royalties. Her husband, with rather a socialistic mind, was a member of the Polish government in exile, and was a very effective agent for his wife's work.

Mr Kuncewicz also started writing his own books. Their large property was partly let, as furnished, and it was my privilege to look after it during their numerous travels around the world.

Did I say privilege? In a way, perhaps it was, but in practice it was a proverbial pain in the neck. Tenants were changing; they had their problems too. I became not only a collector, but a social worker as well. If I did not keep on my toes, who knows what could have happened with some of the tenants? Fortunately, everything was resolved quite amicably.

When Mr and Mrs Kuncewicz were 'at home', we often joined their parties, for the artistic world in London. In their house was a beautiful conservatory, which was an extension to the main building. Lying on the stone floor, there was a Persian carpet, Mr Kuncewicz's pride. He had bought it for next to nothing at an auction. It measured thirty foot by fifteen foot, and was absolutely priceless.

Incidentally, we got to know this family through our window cleaner, Mr Watson; he was also their window cleaner. Mr Watson was a modern day Robin Hood. He would bring us some cutlery from time to time, also from time to time our bits and pieces would disappear.

But Mr Watson would never benefit from any of these transactions.

His son is a professor at Birmingham University. Even now I get a Christmas card, and I always send him forty cigarettes, which unfortunately he adores. This has been a tradition for many years.

Mrs Kuncewicz belonged to the Polish Pen Club, which had an international reputation. We once witnessed her interpretation of *Alice in Wonderland*; it was very well played, especially bearing in mind that few people understand the stories of Lewis Carroll.

Through them we also got to know Mr Topoiski, who was a well-known caricature artist in England, and also on the BBC. I inherited lots of his sketches, and once I went to see his studio under Waterloo Bridge – it was an experience.

Mrs Kuncewicz now lives in their house in Poland, which Jola and I visited in 1976. Mr Kuncewicz died recently. I wonder how the old lady is managing.

The other factor was making the acquaintance of Mr and Mrs Dow, who lived a few houses further along Mayow Road. Alan Dow worked for an export company, in London docks. His wife belonged to a rather well-established family called 'Hands' of south London – Chiselhurst to be precise. Her father was an architect, who had three daughters. They lived a rather secluded life, not being allowed, when single, to travel to central London at all. They had never seen Eros at Piccadilly Circus; in fact they had never travelled on the Underground. We became acquainted with them, and this friendship lasted several years. Mr and Mrs Dow were childless, so they decided to adopt a small boy called Geoffrey, who grew into a very happy and healthy boy.

To this acquaintance, I will return later.

A number of Polish and English friends were still visiting us, which meant that their visits often extended over the weekend.

Meanwhile, Jola's mother, Mrs Stanislawa Wedecka, landed for permanent stay in England. She landed at Hull docks on 29 August 1955. There is a little story attached to her arrival. I travelled to Hull on the first morning train, and not being stopped by anyone, I walked happily to find the particular cargo boat, which had several passenger cabins. I found the boat, but there was no sign of life on the deck. I walked, therefore, on the boat, and found the steward, who was very surprised, and directed me to my mother-in-law's cabin.

No one would believe that I walked freely in the custom-free zone without being stopped. There was a great celebration on the boat, because the other passengers realised that she was the first person who had been allowed to leave Poland permanently since the end of the war.

Later, I was summoned by the Foreign Office officials, it was in fact one of the undersecretaries, who congratulated me personally upon my achievement. In England, my mother came to live with us at Mayow Road. Her possessions were minimal. Unfortunately, she was in a very advanced stage of sclerosis. Most of her joints required immediate treatment, which she received in King's College Hospital, Dulwich.

I will have to skip over many happenings in Mayow Road except one. Mr and Mrs Dow, and their adopted child Geoffrey, were for many years our great friends, and much later we were very proud to attend Geoffrey's wedding in Yeovil. What is very important, is that earlier we were offered an unfurnished flat in Sunderland Road, in the house belonging to Mrs Dow's father, Mr Hands.

We also purchased from Mr Hands several pieces of quite valuable furniture, after accepting the offer of the flat. We now realised that because of the very small rent, we would be able to save a lot of money, which would enable us to buy our own property.

Incidentally, the dining table, chairs and sideboard are now in Ingrid's home; their value has increased quite considerably.

My mother-in-law was making slow progress, which included extensive physiotherapy. I made special handles for her knives, forks and spoons, on the instructions of the hospital. I also constructed rails at home, in order that she could move about. She improved enormously from the condition that she was in on her arrival in England.

Before she fully settled herself in our home, we had a much-deserved holiday in Deal, Kent. We hired a chalet, and the four of us had some very hair-raising experiences. Deal was, in fact, a very uninviting resort for holidays, in my opinion. I remember promising everyone that I would have a daily swim in the sea. I succeeded, but at what a cost! I was literally beaten by the shingle washed off the sea wall before I could reach the water. I used to come out of the water completely mauve. It was extremely interesting to see that Deal, being on the east coast, was separated from the land with a large sea wall. All the holidaymakers would spread themselves and their deckchairs on the west side of the sea defences. There, they would have the benefit of the sun, but without seeing the sea.

We also experienced several thunderstorms, which

almost demolished our chalet. Again, one of our memorable experiences. We were visited by the Cumfts in their van, who were amazed at our holiday; but we all enjoyed it eventually!

The following year, we went to Melford-on-Sea, where we stayed in a hired caravan. That holiday was a little more inviting. The Cumfts came again to see us, and admired the improvements in conditions. This was in 1956.

One of the most memorable holidays of that period was when, in the following year, we went with the Dow family to a rented bungalow in Salcombe. The place was really wonderful, and we enjoyed it as much as we could. Unfortunately, Olgierd became ill with tonsillitis, and this spoiled the second half of his holiday. There was another experience which was difficult to forget – a rowing expedition along the estuary. Without realising it, I was already out in the open channel. It was very fortunate that the tide helped me to row back to the beach. We compensated ourselves by having a lovely tour by motorboat. Everyone, with the exception of Olgierd, was very sunburnt.

Then, in 1959, we went to Monmouth. We visited so many interesting places, including a ride on a narrow-gauge railway; the kind of experience which was not easily forgettable. The ride was followed by a visit to Cardiff.

The following year, our holiday took us to Christchurch, next to Bournemouth and the New Forest. We all did a lot of rowing again, along the river. The area was very picturesque, and we managed not only to visit the New Forest, but also Beaulieu, with Lord Montague's Car Museum, and the remains of the old monasteries. In the New Forest Olgierd had an accident, in that he fell from one of the trees.

We visited the lighthouse opposite the Isle of Wight, at the entry to the Solent. So, too, the Rufus Stone, where King William II, known as Rufus, was slain in 1100. He was shot by Sir Walter Tyrwell. The market in nearby Ringwood was extremely interesting, because at the time you could buy any shotgun, on the market stalls. We also went to the Isle of Wight for the day – it was very lovely.

The following year we spent our holiday at Herne Bay, and this time, Maryla, Tadzik, and my mother paid us a visit.

83 Underhill Road was our first house, which we eventually purchased in March 1959, with a mortgage from Camberwell Borough Council. It was an old house, and ordinary building societies would only give a very small mortgage on this type of property. However, for us it was a great achievement. Actually, with the help of the whole family, we brought it to a reasonable condition, which was improved year by year.

I remember well how everyone contributed in stripping the walls, doors and stairs of numerous layers of paint. I think the stairs had at least six or even seven such layers. The banisters were extremely difficult to strip, and it took us virtually weeks to finish that job. However, it was only the beginning.

It was to everyone's surprise that the whole of the ground floor, was provided with gas lighting of the highest quality. There were brass and crystal chandeliers in all the living rooms; each of these had a pilot gaslight, and all one had to do in the evening was to press the switch on the wall, like one does today with electricity. The house would be immediately illuminated.

The reason for all this luxury was that the owner of the house had been a high-ranking Gas Board official. They had been instructed to have everything where possible connected to gas; they of course paid a special rate. It meant, however, that I had to change all that into an electric system. Sometimes, even today, I am sorry that I disposed of those beautiful chandeliers. The same thing applied to the heating. I had to provide radiators with modern copper pipes.

This also required a new central chimney for the boiler, which I introduced in the kitchen. This was an interesting story, connected with obtaining a waiver to have a five-inch diameter internal flue to such a chimney. The normal requirements specified this should be seven and a half inches in diameter. For the second time, I had to pull out all the stops to find as many possible friends in the GLC, who would find for me a precedent for such a waiver. Eventually, I received a telephone message from County Hall, saying that some years previously, in Middlesex, such a case was fought and the waiver obtained. So the problem was solved, and I built the five-inch diameter chimney, which was quite adequate. As it had been in the corner of the winding staircase, it would mean that the passage of the staircase would be below the required minimum (perhaps another waiver).

There were numerous problems not only with the house, but with the garden as well. The whole site was on a considerable slope upwards towards the back, so much so, that the Overhill Road, which was the parallel street above us, was nearly two storeys above our pavement level.

Once, when I was very ill, with great pains and swollen ankles, I was confined to stay at home for fourteen days. It was a very hot summer, but I decided that I could still do the work outside in the garden, in a sitting position. The soil in our garden was solid clay, which would dry out in the sun until it was hard as stone. Using a chisel and hammer, I sat on a cushion and chopped away, first at the turf, to be used later, and then I removed the wedge-shaped clay over such an area, so that at least we could have something like a twenty-five-foot square, level garden. The clay would have to be broken down, or almost pulverised. I finished the job by placing the turf again. In fourteen days, both my illness and the garden were cured.

It was actually at this time that I was advised to start a claim to the German government for compensation, for the loss of my health during the time spent in the concentration camps. This was done with the help of Dr Alik Domar, who knew me from the time of my liberation and return from Dachau. Also with the help of Dr Held, my GP, and scores of other friends, including Mecenas Clmielewski, they managed to obtain for me a small pension.

At that time, everyone knew that I was suffering from thrombophlebitis in both of my legs, which unfortunately will remain with me for the rest of my life.

My mother was already established permanently in England, and by combining our efforts, we purchased a second-hand VW van in May 1962. I fully converted this van into a motor-caravan; it was, as they say, 'a job and a half'. Not only did I have to cut windows, but I also redesigned the whole of the inside of the van, to serve as a normal vehicle, that could convert from a dining area, during the day, into a double bed for the night.

I had to install a cooker, cupboards and a special

opening in the roof. I completed the job and the van went through a special MOT, with the authorities' approval.

I forgot to tell you that also in Germany, whilst I was in the Polish army, I passed a very strict driving test, which covered almost any type of vehicle, including tanks. However, on my arrival in England, I had forgotten to update my certificate. Consequently, I had to take a driving test in this country. It was to me fortunate, because after a ten year break, and different driving conditions in this country, I became, as I was before, a competent driver. I passed the test first time. It was fortunate that the test examiner had many interests in life similar to my own! Most of my test included conversations about work in the garden; therefore, we missed parts of it!

We decided to go on our first camping holiday, leaving everyone, and everything, behind. Jola and I had the most beautiful touring holiday in Scotland. We were of the opinion that by adopting this country, we should know it well before venturing abroad. In early June, when the days are so long, I took photographs of beautiful sunsets at 11.30 p.m., in Scourie Bay. This part of Scotland was very undulating, and the peat was used for burning in the crofts, during the winter. In this area, we almost lost our motor-caravan; we ventured to go to the seaside, we enjoyed the beach and on our return tried to locate our motor-caravan. We became quite desperate, being unable to see it anywhere; only with the help of a labourer cutting the turf did we find it. Seeing our plight, he indicated where our motor-caravan was located; it was only a stone's throw away from us.

It is interesting that between 1962 and 1986, we had

sixteen different cars. We had a very good principle to change every second or third year, because it was our opinion that this was the only way to have a new car each time.

When Jola was teaching, it was necessary to have two cars. This brings me to a story, from when she was working at the headquarters of the Save the Children Fund. This was from 1962 to 1964 under Colonel Bolton at 29 Queen Anne's Gate. These years were, for Jola, very happy years, and she made scores of friends; she also belonged to the theatre club, so we enjoyed many evenings at different theatres, opera houses and concert halls.

As Jola had failed to continue her medical studies in Woolwich Polytechnic, she decided that firstly, she must improve her English. You remember that both of us entered England without any knowledge of English, and yet the following facts may put a different perspective on her determination for success.

Already in 1948, she had satisfied the University of London requirements for the special university entrance examination. In 1950, Jola had already started on the translation of the books by the well-known Polish writer Jan Dobraczynski, and with his permission translated the first book, *Letters of Nicodemus*. It was fortunate that we got to know Mr Faraker; he was our friend for many years. During the war he had been a censor of all correspondence going between army personnel and their families. His normal job was with the British Museum Library. He agreed to help Jola on her translation work for a very small fee. He was rather eccentric; he went to the barber every day for shaving. But he was a great friend, I must say, and whenever I would be thinking about typical English gentlemen, he was certainly one of them.

As I wrote earlier, in 1967 Jola obtained her BA degree, and after another year at Whitelands College, she obtained her DipEd, which gave her full qualifications to teach. On both occasions, the results were displayed in the Senate House of London University, and I was delegated to see whether she had passed or not. Obviously, the announcements were telephoned by me immediately.

In 1968, she was appointed as a teacher at the Marianne Thornton School in Clapham Common. As her testimonials described, she worked in this school on preparing her girls for O level, and A level English, History and French, all with good results. She also restructured the careers work of the school, made contacts with the Youth Education Board, and through that organisation, placed her pupils in quite good positions (banks, the BBC, etc.). She had regretfully to resign due to ill health in 1972. Her testimonials were signed by Mrs Audrey Cook, the headmistress.

It would be unfair to leave that episode of Jola's work without some light-hearted remarks. Jola realised that travelling from Dulwich to Clapham Common, although not quite four miles, was almost impossible to achieve by London transport, as it would mean making two or three changes, and London buses could run at intervals, varying between twenty and thirty minutes. Therefore, as I mentioned, we decided that Jola would have to pass her driving test, with a view to having another car. She started her driving lessons, still in Kingston, but year after year, she failed. It was the same examiner, each time. Then I decided that we would choose another testing centre, Tottenham, and she had a gentleman examiner, who opened the door for her, and she passed without the slightest hitch.

The problems started when she purchased a second-hand Ford Anglia. On the face of it, everything was all right, but as with all second-hand cars, there were hiccups. The car was very difficult to start; therefore Jola would park it near the school, on a downward slope. Normally it would work all right, but how many times either Olgierd, or myself, would have to go to Clapham Common to give her a push, I cannot remember! Jola did basically enjoy driving; for her it was only a necessity.

I liked her school very much, and the girls from her class would always notice when I drove into school. It always ended in pandemonium, because the continuation of lessons was impossible. I was, of course, always told off. Why was it always my fault? Once Jola organised a special play on King Arthur, Sir Lancelot and Sir Gawain. I had made, a year previously, a puppet theatre for my own children, but however much work and money it cost, it was a complete failure, as they showed an utter lack of interest in it.

However, Jola and her form revived the puppet theatre's value. Everyone was producing puppets, even the Craft Department produced a beautiful axe for chopping the knight's head. I also produced and recorded the music, of which Mozart's Horn Concerto was the greatest success I could expect from any young children. On the whole it was a great success, and Jola was, quite rightly, well congratulated for her efforts.

On another occasion, we had the whole form in our house at Underhill Road. It was a celebration of St Andrew's Day. I could not tell you what enjoyment we all had; the house was buzzing with happy voices, and the climax, well prepared, was the melting of the wax. Each girl would drop into the cold water a spoonful of hot wax, the shadow of which would be projected on to a white screen.

Everyone would have to guess what the shape represented (perhaps it would be her future loved one). A number of girls kept in contact with Jola and myself for a period of several years. Some of them would come to Ixworth and stay for the weekend.

Once, I remember, a lovely Jamaican girl called Joan (now working in King's College Hospital) came to Ixworth by coach, to the great astonishment of the Ixworth inhabitants. They had never seen a black Jamaican. She was a very happy girl – they would talk about her for months.

Even when Jola was so very ill, it was some comfort for her to see those ex-pupils, likewise the visits from her teacher friends. I remember that some time after Jola's death, I contacted one of her pupils, whom I knew very well. By then she was working for the BBC, as a producer for the *Third Programme*. I also knew her parents. I invited her to come and stay at Abbey Cottage, perhaps with her friend. It was to my great astonishment, when the girls arrived, that they were about twenty-eight years old, as I had remembered them as teenagers. Nevertheless, we enjoyed a nice weekend at Ixworth.

From the five years of Jola's teaching, one moment particularly stands out to me. The girls were probably in the third year, when Jola decided to take them to the West End, to the theatre. For some it was nothing special, but for some others, especially the Indian girls it was against their national culture to let the girls go away from home and into the centre of London, without parental escort. Jola had to plead for permission from each parent. Eventually she succeeded, and the parents were promised that the girls would be delivered back home safely.

Some went by bus with the other teacher, but I took some of them in my car to Elephant and Castle Underground Station. There the problems started. The girls had never been on the Underground. Jola was left in the car with some girls, and I took two girls by escalator to the Northern Line platform. I had to hold their trembling hands when the train arrived. It was only three stops, but I had to go with them and get them out at Tooting Underground Station, where they happily departed for their homes. You can imagine Jola with the other girls, waiting for nearly three-quarters of an hour for me, sitting in the car. After my explanations, everything ended happily!

The other incident was when Jola was taken ill, and transported by ambulance from the school to King's College Hospital. Fortunately, her doctor, Professor John Anderson, was there, and the following day she was operated on for gallstones. If I remember rightly, she had thirty-one stones removed.

During the week after the operation, Jola demanded that she must see several girls, who were preparing for their A level examinations. It was only thanks to Professor Anderson that she was allowed to break the hospital rules. The girls came, sat on her bed and did all their revision. Professor Anderson and his ward staff remembered that fact, even to this day.

Afterwards, I took Jola to Aldeburgh for a week, to convalesce. She would sit on the deckchairs every day, regardless of the cold. She stayed with two sisters, who were spinsters; they ran a small cafe, and they looked after her all week, following which I had to return to London to my work.

To complete this stage of Jola's and my life, I must add how pleasant it is, and how proud I am, when looking through the testimonials, starting from Bateman Cleaners in 1951, to Save the Children Fund in 1968, to Woolwich and Kingston Colleges, and finally to the headmistress of Jola's school in Clapham. But most of all I remember the happy faces of the children, who produced one or two tears when their teacher had to retire. There is one story connected with Jola's life, which I will come to a little later.

Holidays, were the time that we should enjoy ourselves as much as possible. It is nice and happy with small children to see how they grow up and enjoy themselves. With the fourteen to sixteen age group one could safely say they would enjoy holiday abroad or even in Britain with the family, but later in life such holidays may be a strain. The last holiday with Olgierd and Ingrid was in our caravan and tent, in August 1964, when we all, including Ingrid's friend Pat, went to France. I was nagged and nagged to reach the south coast as soon as possible, but to their disappointment, all campsites were fully occupied. You could not locate a free space more than two square foot, and the noise from the loudspeakers were deafening, so much so that even our children could not endure it. Therefore, we went on and on, until eventually, on the opposite side of the coast road, the seaside, where the dunes of the disused vineyards were, we found a site. It was peaceful, and to the delight of the girls, was administered by a young and very handsome French farmer. There were explanations from the children: 'Here, here, that will be the best place,' and thank goodness, the children could endure a whole week of that 'heaven'.

Eventually, we departed inland, via Carcasone, a very ancient and beautiful city, to Lourdes. Lourdes, made a very great impression on me (unfortunately Ingrid was taken ill), we visited the sanctuary and watched the regular evening torch procession. The millions of people who visit this place amaze me. What it means to believe in something which may prove to be beneficial to you. This was our last holiday with the children.

Jola and I made several trips to the continent via the Europa Bridge and the Brenner Pass, through the Dolomites, Jessolo, and across the Apennines, and back via Verona, where the Shrine of St Anthony is situated. This we found covered with millions of vows from many ordinary people. They were thanking St Anthony for his help, for a cure or for finding things they had lost. On another occasion, we went to Venice and Florence. It was fortunate that we visited Florence before the floods, as this town is one of the greatest museums in the world, filled with hundreds of works of art.

Ponte Veccio, with its market along the bridge, was a completely unique place. On the way back to England, we went through the tunnel at St Bernard's in the Alps. This was extremely impressive, because we entered the tunnel in almost complete darkness of fog and miserable weather, and on the other side there was beautiful sunshine, something completely unbelievable.

Jola and I had another holiday in France, looking at the chateaus along the Loire River Valley. One of the outstanding places there was the chateau where Leonardo da Vinci spent his last years, with the exhibition of his numerous inventions. The home was given to him by the

Medici family. It was for me a very emotional place.

At the nearby chateau, there was a round tower where in the past, carts pulled by horses would climb to the top terrace, some four storeys above the entrance. The actual holiday was on the west coast next to La Rochelle. From there we went to St Michelle, a most enchanting place full of history.

The last of my holidays with Jola was in Galloway, Scotland, in 1979, where we enjoyed very beautiful summer scenery.

Both mothers settled quite happily in Underhill Road; Mother Wedecka had to visit King's College Hospital very frequently, especially their Physiotherapy Department. However, there was not always such a happy relationship. (My mother-in-law was a natural martyr, whereas, my mother rather liked to impress people.) They both worked very hard. Jola and I managed to divide the work at home in such a way that her mother was in charge of cooking, and my mother would be pottering in the garden for hours. My mother is now in her ninetieth year, and I certainly wish I could be as able to do various works as she is doing now.

In 1972 were the last months of Jola's mother's life, as her strength was waning very rapidly. By that time, I had bought our country cottage in Ixworth, Suffolk; a seventeenth century farmhouse. It was in a terrible condition, and we travelled every weekend to Suffolk 575 times precisely; it was ninety-eight miles from Underhill Road.

We would leave London on Friday evening, work all weekend at the cottage in Suffolk, and then on Sunday evening travel back to London again. One holiday we spent together with our children, in a permanent caravan site opposite the American Base at Lakenheath.

There were some weekends that I was so tired that I had to virtually pinch myself to stay awake to drive. Once, near Newport, I must have dozed off, and it was only landing in a field just before a bend in the road that woke me up. I simply told my passengers that I needed a little rest, and they did not realise what had happened; fortunately, there had not been a ditch.

It is right to make a few digressions, to relieve my story of monotony.

In about 1962, as was written in Olgierd's school report, he was apparently an expert in constructing garages! His schoolmaster was right, because I had decided to build a garage under our ground floor at Underhill Road. It is very much easier to say than to do.

I am a structural engineer, and I had the support of the most famous firm in London and scores of excellent Trollope and Coll workers. I made good practical plans, and had them passed through the local authority. There were a few small problems, like building in front of the existing building line, but with another waiver from the LCC, even that was accomplished.

Charlie Willmont was one of those cockney millionaires who made colossal money on government surplus stock of various machinery. Most importantly for me, on lorries of all shapes and sizes. He purchased them for pennies, then organised a firm and gangs of men to demolish the bombsites in London after the 1942 blitz. That was an enormous job. In addition, he also undertook the straight excavations for the future buildings. He knew all his workers by their Christian names, and they all knew him as Charlie.

Charlie drove a Rolls Royce, and there were always

tape recorders, and cameras sticking out of his pockets. He had a good word for everyone, and was extremely helpful. Once, I approached him and asked whether he would be willing to help me, but I said, 'No favours – I will pay for the work.' We were very good friends.

'Mr K, what is the problem?' he asked me.

I replied, 'I want to build a garage under my house, but I have to remove about sixty cubic yards of soil, which is the way to make the opening.' I showed him the plans.

His answer was very simple. 'Is £25 OK? I will send my surveyor straight away, and the job will be done as soon as possible.'

His surveyor came, measured everything up and said, 'Will this Saturday be all right?'

I replied, 'Yes.'

On Saturday morning, most of our neighbours had gone to work, when at about 9 a.m. a large lorry with a digger arrived, with four large empty lorries and about ten men with shovels and picks. Within the width of the drive, the solid front wall was removed. Within two hours, eighty cubic yards of clay had been carried away. The site was cleaned, and before I could realise, the three-storey wall with the ground floor window above was totally exposed, leaving hardly any space to enter the house. I received the bill for £25 one month later! You can imagine my neighbours' responses when they returned at midday; nobody could believe that this was possible.

The next problem was that I had to cut an opening in the lower part of the front wall, for the entry into the future garage. I also had to build the side walls, and steps leading to the house.

Again I went to a good friend, the foreman on the Kingsway job, and laid before him the problem. I told him, 'I need first to underpin the front wall.'

'OK,' he replied, 'it will be done.' Four men, shovels, a lorry, a few bags of cement and gravel, and the job was completely carried out. Then I proceeded to cut a slot in the main wall, on two sides and under the ground floor. To do this I needed steel needles and reinforcement for the future lintel. You should have seen the people when, with the light in the basement, they could only see three steel needles and a continuous slot supporting the whole of the front wall; it was frightening.

Once, I remember, I was watched by a man sitting on a wall on the other side of the road. He could not help it – he came across the road, and asked me very politely whether I knew what I was doing. 'To be quite frank,' I replied, 'I don't.'

He said, 'I am an architect, and you cannot mess about like this without some professional advice; it is extremely dangerous, what you are doing.'

'Never mind,' I replied. 'I am myself a structural engineer with many years of practice, and I have given advice to many architects on much more important problems. Therefore, don't worry.'

'I am very sorry,' said the man, and I did not see him again.

The next job was reinforcing and concreting the lintel beams, and the roof slab of the projection in front of the building. Help came again from a couple of men and some ready-mixed concrete, and one Saturday the lintel and the slab, with adequate shattering and reinforcement, were completed.

On Monday, I remember I had a telephone call from

Jola, that two young men claiming to be assistants from the District Surveyor's office, were jumping on the roof to test it. This made me furious. I telephoned the District Surveyor, whom I knew well, and I had no more interference. Fortunately, the future ground floor of the garage was still above the street level, and about six inches above the old drain – what luck!

The last thing was to construct a large sliding door. I went to my timber contracting section, we fixed a price, and a beautifully-constructed door arrived on time.

There remained only the finishing touches, like an asbestos ceiling to prevent fire, and similarly, self-closing fireproof doors. Externally, there was a steel balustrade, for bending the tubular sections. I used the drain covers.

There is only one small postscript to what I have written earlier, that my garage projected about four foot in front of the building line. I managed to get a waiver for that. In a year or two most houses like mine built similar garages; it was extremely pleasing to me.

Now I would rather return to the stories of our children. Olgierd passed his entrance examination to Dulwich College, but unfortunately it was for a fee-paying place, which we could not afford. Dulwich College was, and still is, very exclusive, and was attended by the sons of ambassadors, sheiks and royalty who would have the pleasure of their children obtaining the Dulwich Certificate.

It is very worthwhile to note that the original Dulwich College was established in 1619, for twelve poor scholars of the area. In 1887, Alleyns had grown to 250 boys and had to move to its present premises.

Nevertheless, there was an agreement between Dulwich College and Alleyns School (the latter being the original Dulwich College) that Alleyns would take some of the boys who would satisfy entrance examination for the free places, using government grant. This was regarded as a Direct Grant School.

Our interview and Olgierd's with the headmaster was successful, and he started his secondary education in 1963, joining Henderson House at Alleyns. His housemaster, Mr Barker, was an ideal teacher; he knew Olgierd very well, and admired his inventiveness, diligence and basically good behaviour, for the whole duration, until reaching the O and A levels.

Olgierd liked football, but most of all fives. He was always interested in photography – he obtained an award for one of his trick photographs – and he was excellent at woodwork. He enjoyed cadets, camping and canoeing; this was probably why he liked the north of England, as all his camps, some of which were very arduous, were there.

His O level results were excellent, especially considering how little work it cost him. The A levels, as Mr Barker had predicted, were rather difficult, and I sometimes had to help him. He was generally a strong, healthy boy he loved cycling, swimming and eventually, with a rather less happy face, he obtained a place at York University.

Whilst still in Alleyns he was faced with one great disappointment. He applied for training at the Royal Naval School for Flying – sadly, he was rejected in 1967. The reason given was that his parents were of foreign birth. We appealed but without success.

However, to finish this chapter in a lighter mood, I will say a little more about something which was my great pleasure – music.

An incident related to my ability to sing, was that in

London, Jola and I attended several concerts, including that of Boris Godunow in Covent Garden, sung by Boris Christoff. At the same time our neighbours in Underhill Road, Mr and Mrs Cricmere, attended all promenade concerts in the Albert Hall every year. They applied for tickets for the last night of the Proms, which could only be given after a ballot, in which they were successful.

Unfortunately, nearly one month before that concert, we received a telephone call from his wife, saying that he was critically ill in St George's Hospital, after suffering a heart attack whilst at a concert. When we arrived at the hospital, it was only moments before he died.

Subsequently, the tickets for the last night of the Proms arrived to their house; what an irony! However, Mrs Cricmere decided that Jola and I must go instead. We graciously accepted, and fully enjoyed the magnificent experience of Sir Malcolm Sergeant, conducting the last Prom of the season. We had Mr Cricmere in our minds all the time.

Whenever I look back to that evening, I am sure that of all occasions when I have had the luck to be in that building, the memorial to Prince Albert built by Queen Victoria, that particular one was the most memorable. There was one incident connected with that evening. We had parked our car in one of the side streets. On our return, the cars behind and in front were parked bumper to bumper with our motor-caravan. It took me two hours to get our vehicle out, moving backwards and forwards, inch by inch!

In 1966, we went on holiday to Wales, in a caravan camp, with our newly acquired dog, a chow, called Meme. We experienced very bad weather, and it poured with rain most of the time.

After one week, we decided that, enough was enough, and we moved across country to the east, to East Anglia. We landed in Ely. We admired the cathedral, and for some unknown reason, we started looking in the estate agents' windows.

We realised there could be a chance for us to buy a small property, where we could go for long weekends or even for our holidays. We started suddenly to look for such an object in earnest. After several attempts in the area of Ely, Thetford and Newmarket, we landed in Bury St Edmunds. At the agency of Lacy Scott, we were told by a young assistant, that there was an old seventeenth century cottage in Ixworth, which might be of some interest to us. I don't think they were very serious!

So we came to Ixworth and, whether it was the picturesque cottage, the hollyhocks in full bloom or our eagerness to carry out another piece of pioneering work, but one of these points made us believe that this cottage was what we wanted. We returned to Lacy Scott's offices, and made our offer. The offer was accepted the next day by Mr John Cross, and after a long period of our solicitor in London, and their solicitor in Bury St Edmunds negotiating the purchase, the transaction was concluded in October 1966.

We had already shown the property to both our children and mothers. There was a mixed reception to our idea, but eventually everyone accepted it.

As I said somewhat earlier, we eventually travelled every weekend from London to Ixworth, until the final move in 1972, some six years and over 300 trips later.

I don't know whether this was again an act of providence that we bought the place. After all, we did not know that the tragic end of Jola's mother would eventually be in Ixworth. We certainly did not anticipate Jola's illness, as she was then still quite healthy. Regardless, for the difficulties we had to face, it proved so beneficial that I am certain that Jola would not have survived her cancer for so many years if we had stayed in London. After all, she managed to give so much of herself to so many! She managed to make so many people happy, making her struggle worth the effort.

I made very detailed plans of the property, and studied its construction and the possibilities of saving as much of it as was possible. The cottage was built in 1622 or 1623.

My first visit was to Mr Kanyon, who was responsible for the development and conservation of the Bury St Edmunds area. He told me that 'Abbey Cottage', as our new property was called, was a listed building, because of the very impressive seventeenth century chimney. I agreed with him, but I was also relieved to learn that some other parts, which were already much deteriorated, could be pulled down. This I did almost single-handed.

I had then only some help from our neighbours from across the road, Mr and Mrs Mower, and their son Derek. Harold Mower was a gamekeeper for the Crofts family, and one part of our cottage had been used as a shooting lodge. There were still some stuffed pheasants and grouse there. The family was extremely nice, and helped us enormously. For the first six years, the key was with them, and any activities were always done with their help and advice.

Unfortunately, Harold died very soon from a heart attack. It was a great blow to the whole family, but especially to his wife Barbara. She suffered for years with rheumatism, and at one time, Harold had to help her dress and put her to bed. She has now recovered remarkably, perhaps, as a result of her long and frequent visits to her children in the USA, especially during the late autumn and winter.

I made plans for how I was going to alter the building, and submitted them to the local authorities in Bury St Edmunds. Mr Holmes was the Health Inspector for the then Thingoe Council, and he had been responsible for the closure order on the cottages before we purchased them; this was for health reasons. He was very helpful to us, and gave me much advice about how to go on with repairs and alterations so that the closure order could be lifted.

After asking several local firms to give me an estimate for doing this work, I had to agree to a small London firm, whom I knew earlier, to do the job, for a fixed sum of money. I had no end of trouble with these people and their workmen. As a result, I had to send them off, and slowly do the work myself with the help of casual workers, one of whom was a very good local man called Fred Lilley. The London firm and their associates eventually went bankrupt negotiating the purchase – I was not surprised.

Had I known the other firms better, which gave estimates based on an undetermined hourly basis, as I know them today, certainly they would have been given the job, and I am sure in the end, it would have cost me much less. However, my financial resources were rather limited.

The cost of reconstructing those two cottages (there were two of them, semi-detached), when looking back, was colossal: but the pleasure of doing what I wanted, and making it how I wanted it to be, was overwhelmingly in favour of the decision I had taken.

After all, I am an experienced structural engineer. Only I could say what the structural alterations could be made, and how.

During my practice in Bury St Edmunds, I did the design of the reconstruction of the Unitarian Church in Churchgate Street. It was an extremely difficult job to refurbish and correct this early Victorian building, and I did, in the words of the architect, Mr Martin Whitworth, 'a very satisfactory job, in extremely difficult circumstances'.

I therefore applied my knowledge to my cottage, and I was pleased with the results. This was the most important thing to me.

There were two things we did almost at the very beginning. The first was to enclose our property with a fence. It was a tremendous length, but we purchased so many dozens of six-foot-square interwoven fencing panels, that no one here would believe that we would ever need. With the help of Harold Mower, the posts were concreted into dug-out holes, and we erected the fence on the west side.

But hold on for a moment – it was not so easy to determine that line. All that was described in the deeds was the length of the frontage, and this I measured and instructed our solicitor to include this in our deeds, but the west side was not so easy to determine.

During the time when we were originally setting out the fence line, someone came and told us, 'That is wrong – there was a path and another kissing gate, where I used to court my wife.' (There was another, similar gate opposite.) I had to go to John Cross and explain the problem – he of course agreed, and I gained a substantial area of ground, plus a lovely apple tree.

After erecting the fence, I decided to plant some trees.

It was not a good decision. I planted about twenty or twenty-five poplar trees. Only two or three remain now (twenty years hence).

Then we went to the large local nursery of Mr Barcock, near Drinkstone. It was on his advice that we planted laurels along the west fence. But there was a catch. I was told to dig a four-foot-wide and two-foot-deep trench, along the whole 300 foot, and place at least 8 yards of manure, covered with topsoil, well in advance of planting the laurels. He was right, the laurels looked splendid, but you can imagine the work, the smell and the time sacrificed to this task. Everybody was sympathetic about my efforts, and not so pleased with the farmyard smell.

Barcock's nursery supplied us with roses, trees and dahlias, which were once the pride of our garden, and admired by many.

After all these years, when I look back, I realise looking at the original photographs that our garden has changed very much. Once even, when I was away, and left two youngsters to clear the area – and it was understood by them to mean that I wanted them to cut down the trees – even after the removal of those trees, this garden is still rich in foliage and blooms, and there are still many trees.

I am sorry that I lost our Christmas tree, which we transferred from London.

Trollope and Colls had various jobs for me in the city of London, and their foremen helped me quite a lot. That is the reason why so many items, like doors, windows, fireplaces, central heating and many other items, were purchased and delivered to Ixworth with their help. Often when they were on the way to

Cambridge, or other contracts external to London, those items would be dropped off here. I do not think I could ever have managed without their help.

The other person local in Ixworth is Fred Lilley. He is a bricklayer by trade, but works now as a fore-man/manager for an agricultural firm in Stanton. He built many internal brick walls for me, of the very old two-inch thick bricks, which I collected from that part of the cottage that I had originally pulled down. He did lots of repairs to outside rendering, and applied a Tyrolean finish to the whole exterior, in Suffolk pink. I am greatly in the debt of Fred, and Kitty his wife, who, not being well herself, suffered many times because of waiting for Fred to come from Abbey Cottage, sometimes very late. Nevertheless, he also likes our cottage, and whenever he can, even now, comes and offers his help for very little reward. Thank you, Fred, it is much appreciated!

I have to recall one day, at the very start of my recon-struction work. As I said earlier, I pulled down one wing of the cottages. This was almost beyond repair. However, there was also incorporated an old chimney stack. I had borrowed a very large differential pulley arrangement and some long strong rope from my firm in London. I anchored one end of this to the tree trunk in the garden, and the other end to the chimney stack. I strained it as much as I could, but it would not give in. Therefore, I applied the old-fashioned method of pulling the strained rope. I introduced a swing action in an attempt to pull down the chimney stack (you may remember my demolition work in the Warsaw ghetto). It did not work. The workers on an adjoining building site saw my struggle, and came to the rescue. The chimney stack was, eventually, brought down, and I was very thankful to those men!

It is very important to me, and this is well documented, in our photographic records, how many jobs on this cottage were carried out.

I could, in fact, write a whole chapter on this subject, but let's concentrate on a few aspects:

The cottage – actually, there were two cottages joined, forming a 'K' shape. As I said earlier I was permitted to pull some parts down, leaving the main chimney intact. Whether I made the right or the wrong decision, it is too late to comment. However, the oldest wing was pulled down. It was a mammoth operation, I felt like Samson, dismantling some of the roof's oak beams, and toppling over to the ground. After pulling the chimney down, I had the huge task of clearing the site, and to collect all the valuable two-inch bricks. These were handmade, about four centuries ago.

I know that I was a strong man, but hitherto I had never realised the practical application of that strength of mine. The amount of work I carried out in those few years was, when looking back, astonishing.

One example will demonstrate this. When the roof was re-covered with concrete pantiles of the Grovebury type, I noticed that the only valley was done in ordinary felt, and not in lead-bedded timber boards as specified.

The lead was brought in a handsome roll, well over a hundredweight. The timber boards were also provided, and after stripping part of the roof on either side of this valley, I fixed the boards, and when looking at the workmen, I realised that no one was capable of laying the lead bedding. There was only one way – I had to put this roll of lead, on to my shoulder and climb, first on the ladder, and then along the laid boards, to the roof top. There I nailed the end of the lead roll, and let it unroll itself down the valley of the roof. A little adjustment and nailing it to the boards completed the job – may I say, to the amazement of the onlooking helpers! This way of doing the necessary work was repeated many times.

Looking back at the slow transformation of Abbey Cottage into quite a respectable, and I should say, desirable property in Ixworth, I sometimes wonder where I managed to get the inspiration and resources necessary to do all that work. Our budget was built on the shoestring principle.

However, every so often I would undertake major alterations, to the things which had once been done and altered before. I remember Fred coming, and being in complete despair at my new ideas. The only thing which persuaded him to provide the necessary help was the fact that I, as an engineer, understood the problem. He also knew that I would never do something which would prove to be unsafe.

I do not think that there is even one item in Abbey Cottage which was not altered at least once. From pure necessity, many parts of the cottage were altered up to four times. Perseverance was the theme then!

There are many items in Abbey Cottage which were designed and built by myself and which are unique to that type of 1640s timber structure, but at the end of my book would like to list at least four of them:

1) A large inglenook fireplace with a copper hood, designed and made by myself.

2) A handmade steel spiral staircase.

3) Within that stairwell there was enough space to accommodate a two-person fully automatic lift,

built of hardwood construction and protected by a wired glass surround. I designed the both the machinery and the controlling mechanism. Jola's health was deteriorating rapidly and she was not able to use the stairs, and this gave me the incentive to build that lift.

This lift was the only structure of its kind in Ixworth, or even East Anglia, and was even mentioned in the press.

4) The main stairs were also designed and made by myself from very old, well-seasoned teak. Again, the design was to match the interior of that special cottage.

When I had almost completed reconstructing the old fourteenth century derelict cottage I was a very happy man.

I feel that I am entering the last stage of my life with a clear slate; with a feeling that all those struggles were worthwhile, and that they are now behind. Knowing that even if there are problems, crises and disappointments, there also will be tears of happiness and the great satisfaction of each and every new achievement. That is what life is about!

Printed in the United Kingdom
by Lightning Source UK Ltd.
118228UK00001B/22-33